AUDITING HUMOR

and other
OXYMORONS

Mike Jacka

DEDICATION

To my parents,
This is as much your fault as anyone's.

ACKNOWLEDGEMENTS

(Sorry, this is almost serious. But even auditors sometimes develop chinks in their hearts of feldspar.)

I've been incredibly lucky to work with and around people who, within reason, let me be as strange as I wanted to be. It all started with Sue Neal and Dave Sanders who still talk about the second audit report I ever wrote (second draft) about the 88 account fairies who spread IBM cards throughout the department for all the clerks to work on. (IBM cards...man, that was a long time ago.)

After that, there are a lot of people who had some responsibility (culpability) for helping shape whatever this is. In no particular order: Steve Gawlowski (back then we couldn't turn to the internet to look up Bubble Puppy), Chuck Boyer, Kathy Otis, Greg Dahinden, Beth Jordan, Jeff Hadley, Misty Mantzey, Syd Holtan (always be nice, you never know who you are going to work for), Allen Engel, Marilee Lemmon, Ken Carroll (who, I think, never quite understood, but let me go crazy anyway), James Hansen, Russell Powers, Mark Brinkley, Bob Keto (none of us can express how much we all still miss him), Tami Wolf, Larry Lott, Dan Clemens, sheesh, I know I've missed a bunch.

(And, no, you don't all get free copies)

And a special thanks, as always, to Paulette Keller. She is a great friend, a fantastic co-worker, and a person-who-allows-all-kind-of-strange-ideas-to-be-bounced-off.

None of this would have been possible without the incredible staff at Internal Auditor magazine. They gave me almost carte blanch to try and figure out what funny internal auditing meant. (And later they actually got me an award. I understand the recounts are still going on.) It all started with Anne Graham who published my first article. But the humor pieces really exist because of Anne Millage, Dave Salierno, Tim McCollum, and Joanne Hodges (they're the ones who had to edit most of these messes), as well as everyone else who ever worked on the staff.

And, you've got to thank family right? Well, at least I do. I dedicated this to my parents (who are now changing their names and trying to find a nice little chateau in Nepal in which to hide), but let me throw a thank you in there, too. Also, thanks to my sister who put up with me almost as long as my parents did. And a special thanks to my wife (30+ years, and she is still pretending to think I'm funny) and my kids. (Sally, Dan, I'm really sorry for how warped you became being raised this way.)

And, not that they will ever notice or ever care, but a thank you to all the strange influences in my life: Wallace and Ladmo, Warren Zevon, Harlan Ellison, SpongeBob SquarePants, Roger Ramjet, Goose Creek Symphony, the Smothers Brothers, Walt Disney, Rocky and Bullwinkle, the Dick Van Dyke Show, Mike Nesmith, and a whole lot more you probably wouldn't recognize anyway. (You've got internet access; look 'em up.)

And, finally, a thank you to anyone who has the chutzpah and questionable taste to have purchased and enjoyed this book. Thanks for being a little off plumb and for recognizing that even internal auditing can be funny.

Table of Contents

Auditing
THE MUSICAL

You may have felt your dark side overtaking you until you saw a musical about a phantom. You may have thought your life was miserable until you saw a musical about the French Revolution. You may have thought a musical about cats was purr-fect. But now, take a risk, throw out your schedule, and prepare to add value to your life – "Auditing: The Musical" has spread across the landscape. Broadway is still buzzing about the debut performance of "The Audit."

Based on the changing role of auditing, the story centers on three individuals – Mary, John, and Rick. After the rousing overture, a snap-step group of auditors in dark three-piece suits sing the Sousaesque march, "We're Bayoneting the Wounded," while stabbing imaginary bodies with six-foot long mechanical pencils.

They are led by Rick, an old guard auditor, who goes on to sing "The Con of Consulting," a troubling song that describes consulting as a fool's game – affirming that the success of auditing will always be measured by the bodies left in its wake.

As the group of auditors leaves happily slapping each other on the back, John hangs behind. A young auditor with visions of adding value dancing in his head, he sits and sings the haunting melody, "An Auditor Is Not an Animal":

"Things are different in the real world, Am I a good guy or a bad?
Some say that I'm a savior, Others spit and call me cad."

Soon, we are introduced to Mary – a new, bright-eyed auditor with a can-do attitude. She meets Rick on her first day where he trains her to the strains of "The Tick-and-Tie Polka":

"Add this here and crossfoot there – check the numbers everywhere,
If there's a problem scream and swear. The Tick-and-Tie Polka."

Mary is quickly enraptured by Rick and the exciting world of auditing he portrays – one filled with head counts and terminations left in his wake. But at a party the next night, she meets John. As they dance to the "Workpaper Waltz," John has the opportunity to talk to her about how auditing is changing. As he reprises the first two lines of "An Auditor Is Not an Animal,"

"Things are different in the real world, Am I a good guy or a bad?"

a chorus of dancers in the background continues to chant, "We're Bayoneting the Wounded."

Then, off in the distance for the first time, we hear the strains of "Brave New Auditing World":

"I can smell the winds of change, in everything we do,
In ICQs and spreadsheets. Can you smell it to?"

From here on, scene after scene demonstrates the constant struggle between the old and new worlds of auditing. Mary, symbolically caught between these worlds in her feelings for Rick and John, is trying to make choices between collaboration and body counts, change and the status quo, and, ultimately, right and wrong.

There are a number of blindingly memorable songs, including a hilarious send-up of hip-hop music called "The Methods of Sampling," which includes electronic samples of business machines providing the rhythm and percussion; "Original Work," a blues number lamenting the inability of auditors to have an original idea; and "We're Here to Help You," which is sung by the group of auditors as they enter the accounting department to begin the audit.

The showstopper comes just before intermission as Mary pours her heart out in the searing anthem, "The Risk of Being Wrong."

> *"Inherent in the risk is the thought it might be true.*
> *Controlling myself from the risk of loving you.*
> *The detection of these risks has taken me too long,*
> *Now I'm running the risk of being wrong."*

Finally, the conflict reaches its climax as Rick, John, and Mary hold their wrap-up meeting with the accounting department. Getting the final results has been a struggle as John and Rick fight for different interpretations of the facts. In "Findings or Observations," a piece equal to Mozart's best, the theatergoer is treated to a half-hour of intertwining melodies. First, John and Rick sing a duet, arguing their points in front of the client.

Rick: *"You know the clerk didn't do her job!"*
John: *"But, tell me, was she trained?"*
Rick: *"90 of 100 wrong!!"*
John: *"But can you feel her pain?"*

Mary joins the two in a soul-searching aria, providing a counterpoint of divided loyalties, mortified that this struggle is happening before the auditee:

> *"Customer or client, there's no need they see this riot.*
> *Though I struggle with who's right and who is wrong."*

The director of the accounting department then weaves a new theme, questioning what he is seeing, but seemingly understanding John's points much more than Rick's:

> *"Please don't find my foibles, ignore my slips and errors.*
> *But if you must report them, please pretend you care."*

At this point, Mary realizes she has called the auditee a "customer." The dawning of enlightenment grows on her face as her melody begins a slow but deliberate weave with John's heart-warming voice.

Meanwhile, Rick's song becomes harsher and more dissonant. Soon, the director of accounting's refrain also slides in tune with John and the two begin singing the uplifting "What Control Means to Me."

Rick is beaten, and, as a chorus made up of the entire accounting department gives its support to John's understanding of the audit process, Rick slinks away to the dark wings of stage left. The entire ensemble – John and Mary now arm in arm – joins in a triumphant "Brave New Auditing World":

> *"Feel it deep within you, like a thunderstorm it rolls.*
> *Like the clouds it covers everything, like the mighty wind it blows."*

I defy you to go to a performance that does not end with a half-hour of standing ovations and curtain calls. Never has the world of auditing been so mesmerizingly portrayed against the backdrop of torn human emotions. If I communicate no other result, let it be that, in my opinion, "Auditing – The Musical" is a smash, and it is my recommendation that everyone see it as a corrective action against the boredom of everyday life.

THE ADVENTURES OF

AUDITORMAN
AND
COSO BOY

[Cue sinister background music.]

NARRATOR: In a city with no controls. [Gunfire] In a town full of risks. [A woman's scream] In a time where efficiency and effectiveness have no meaning. [Sirens] Is there no one who is independent and objective? Is there no one to consult with? Is there no one to provide assurance? Do not fear, citizens. There is... Auditorman and COSO Boy!

[Cue "The Auditorman March"]

NARRATOR: The Adventures of Auditorman and COSO Boy are brought to you by The Committee of Sponsoring Organizations of the Treadway Commission – "A new cube for every decade" – and by The IIA – "What happens in auditing, stays in auditing, and in the audit committee."

By day, Auditorman is Marvel Kenlay, social gadabout, flagrant flaunter of audit conventions, and chief executive officer of Marvel Marketing. COSO Boy is Jeff Skilless, Kenlay's naive but headstrong administrative assistant. Endless days immersed in the boring world of sales promotions are brought to a halt when evil rears its ugly head. Then they shed that grey existence for the fast-paced, ever-changing world of auditing.

Defenders of truth, justice, and The IIA's professional standards, Auditorman and COSO Boy use due professional care to assess the city, identifying opportunities for improvement and following-up to ensure action plans are appropriately executed.

When last we saw our heroes, they had just wrapped up the Case of the Unsupported Finding. Commissioner Richards speaks.

COMMISSIONER: I thought for sure you were goners, Auditorman. Dr. Detail had so much information. I would have bet money you and COSO Boy would be buried forever.

AUDITORMAN: No commissioner. Yes, he had a lot of information, but there was no analysis. It was easy enough to dig ourselves out of his devilish detour when it became apparent his findings were built on suspect information and false documentation.

COSO BOY: Holy workpapers, Auditorman. It looked like the proof was there. But it just didn't hold up to your scrutiny. If it hadn't been for you, it might have been reported that controls were insufficient. And the report would have been ...

Wrong.

[Organ sting]

AUDITORMAN: Well, little chum, I don't want to take all the credit. It's only through the help of everyone in the professional Audit Hero Community that we can succeed against evil. Our books would have been cooked without the help of the Fantastic Five: Mr. Environment, RA the Magnificent, Activity Lass, Monitor Lizard, and the Information and Communication Twins.

COMMISSIONER: Doesn't that make six?

COSO BOY: Holy reconciliation, commissioner. Don't stop him now; he's on a roll.

AUDITORMAN: Yes, the seeds of poor governance bear bitter fruit, and the fruit of bad controls results in a sticky syrup of incorrect financial statements. But Dr. Detail is not the real problem. Nor are the other minions of evil such as The Inefficiency Expert, the Governless Governor, and The Financial Statement Falsifier. They are but tools in a neverending quest to leave us powerless in our sacred duty of ensuring objectives are met. Our true nemesis is Captain Chaos–Control Crusher – the spawn of all breakdowns. Why, I remember ...

COMMISSIONER: Excuse me, Auditorman. [Phone receiver clicks.] Commissioner Richards here ... No! It can't be. Wait. Let me put you on the Speaker Phone of Pertinent Communication. [phone static] Agent QA, Auditorman and COSO Boy are here with me. Tell them what you told me.

AGENT QA: We've gotten a demand letter from The Fraudster.

COSO BOY: Holy embezzlement, Auditorman. Not the Fraudster!

AUDITORMAN: I'm afraid so, little chum. Go on, Q. What is that vile bender of truth demanding?

AGENT QA: Apparently, The Fraudster has captured one of our super audit heroes and is demanding a ransom. He's holding…The Duty Segregator.

[Organ sting]

COMMISSIONER: Noooooooo!

COSO BOY: Holy collusion, Auditorman. That means people will start combining incompatible functions, doing both jobs in a flagrant disregard for appropriate controls.

AGENT QA: It gets worse, COSO Boy. They've also captured ... The Approver.

[Organ sting]

COMMISSIONER: Nooooooooo!

AUDITORMAN: Is there no end to this madman's reign of terror? The

Fraudster's affecting both preventive and detective controls.

AGENT QA: Auditorman, he's demanding that you and COSO Boy meet him at the old mail-shipping warehouse on the wharf.

COSO BOY: Holy scope creep, Auditorman. It's a trap.

AUDITORMAN: No doubt of it, little chum. But, if I've analyzed the data correctly, that is only part of his nefarious scheme. If he is lurking at the mail-shipping warehouse, then that means the mail system is about to be the first victim of this dastardly plan.

AGENT QA: You're right, Auditorman. The Fraudster has removed all governance controls over the mail system. Our mail may not be sent on time.

[Organ sting]

COMMISSIONER: Noooooooo!

AUDITORMAN: To the Riskmobile, COSO Boy!

NARRATOR: Auditorman and COSO Boy leap into the Riskmobile. [A jet engine sounds and tires squeal.] They speed through the city taking an efficient path to what appears to be a blank brick wall. [An engine revs harder] Plunging headlong into the dead-end alley, it appears they are headed for certain doom when the wall opens up and they drive into the darkness. [The sound of the engine and tires ends abruptly.] Deep within the basement of the Marvel Building is hidden the Secure Lair of Secretiveness – where Auditorman and COSO Boy maintain their ever-vigilant review of the city. [Footsteps … then the sound of electrical equipment being turned on.]

AUDITORMAN: Let's get to work, COSO Boy. We have a lot of analysis to do. Laptops on.

COSO BOY: Check.

AUDITORMAN: Spreadsheets open.

COSO BOY: Check.

AUDITORMAN: Red Book handy.

COSO BOY: Check.

AUDITORMAN: Mechanical pencils at hand.

COSO BOY: Holy just-in-time inventory, Auditorman. We've got a lot of work to do. We may not have enough lead for our mechanical pencils.

AUDITORMAN: We'll just have to make do, old chum. We'll just have to make do.

[Organ sting]

NARRATOR: Auditorman and COSO Boy begin work to ensure they have a plan of attack – creating files and folders where all the documentation can reside, designing tests to ensure their plans are adequate, and documenting every step of their laborious research into the plans of The Fraudster. Day turns into night. They check and cross-foot, tic and tie, and photocopy and scan. Night turns to day, and back into night. Five days later, they leap back into action, firing up the Riskmobile. [An engine roars to life and tires squeal.] Negotiating their way through the city, they finally find themselves in the darkened warehouse. [The engine turns off. In the background a buoy bell rings and there is the occasional forlorn sound of a foghorn. A large solid door creaks open, thuds shut, and there is the sound of footsteps.]

COSO BOY: [Whispering] Holy security, Auditorman. How did we slip in so easily?

AUDITORMAN: No doubt, they want us here. Observe every step of your progress, COSO Boy. There are bound to be traps. [More footsteps. Suddenly, the sound of a projectile flying through the air.] Look out, COSO Boy! The scoundrel has us under attack. [The sound of more projectiles, slowly at first, then more and more]

COSO BOY: Holy ICQ, Auditorman. What is it?

AUDITORMAN: Those are signed agreements, each one promising more and more return. And each one liable to inflict a particularly nasty paper cut.

COSO BOY: There's not that many, Auditorman. Can't we just attack?

AUDITORMAN: Not so fast, chum. Notice they are coming faster and faster. [The sound of the projectiles continues to increase.] We are under attack by a classic Ponzi scheme.

COSO BOY: Holy pyramid, Auditorman. If we don't do something soon, it will all collapse around us!

THE FRAUDSTER: I've got you now, you caped control freaks. Give up and I might be willing to keep you on as my accountants.

COSO BOY: Never, Fraudster. We'd never stoop that low.

AUDITORMAN: Never fear, little chum. Let me just check my utility belt here…Yes! I've got it. Stand back. [A loud explosion and the groan of an injured man]

COSO BOY: What was that, Auditorman?

AUDITORMAN: I hit the lying scoundrel with a confirmation bomb. His scheme collapsed right back on him. Let's go interrogate. [Footsteps] Fraudster, what have you done with The Duty Segregator and The Approver?

CAPTAIN CHAOS: Auditorman. COSO Boy. I've been waiting.

COSO BOY: Holy framework, Auditorman. It's Captain Chaos–Control Crusher.

CAPTAIN CHAOS: Right you are, COSO Dork. And you are now standing exactly where I need you. [A large roar – the sound of paper flooding down a chute.]

COSO BOY: Auditorman! What is it?

CAPTAIN CHAOS: It's the mail, COSO Dweeb. An entire day's worth of mail. [A diabolical laugh] Without approvals and without separation of duties, I was able to ensure that the day's worth of mail went undelivered. And now, you are both trapped.

COSO BOY: Holy corrective action, Auditorman. What will we do?

AUDITORMAN: I'm not sure yet, COSO Boy. And our dilemma is much worse than you may have realized. Do you know what today is?

CAPTAIN CHAOS: Let me guess, Auditornerd. The day you finish your last audit? The day you come to your concluding conclusion? The day of your final final report?

AUDITORMAN: None of those. COSO Boy, today is the day our CPE reports are due.

COSO BOY: Holy certification, Auditorman. You don't mean ...

AUDITORMAN: I'm afraid so little chum. If that mail doesn't go out today, we can no longer use our CIA designations.

[Organ sting]

NARRATOR: What's to become of Auditorman and COSO Boy? Is this their exit interview? Will they ever get out from under the crush of daily mail? Will their CPE reports get to headquarters in time? Will they be forced to change their business cards by removing their CIA designations? Join us next week for the answers to these and even more close-ended questions on ...

THE ADVENTURES OF AUDITORMAN AND COSO BOY

[Cue "The Auditorman March" and fade.]

CHEZ AUDITING

Good evening and welcome to Chez Auditing. You are about to embark on a unique dining experience that combines the joy of fine food with the thrill of quality auditing. Our charter is to provide an independent, objective, and risk-reduced dining environment where we partner with you to ensure we are all successful. At Chez Auditing, we are truly here to serve you.

I am Maurice, and I will be your maitre d' – the lead if you will. It is my duty to provide you initial notification of what you can expect throughout this evening's engagement. I will lay out our plans for your evening and explain what we will need to make it a success. Together, we will determine the scope of your meal.

Unfortunately, we currently find ourselves in ever-greater demand. After all, just down the street, the smash musical SOX It to Me continues to play to sold out crowds. Accordingly, although we planned to start right away, we must now ask you to wait. However, this delay will in no way increase your personal exposures. Instead, what better way to get to know us than to visit our cocktail lounge, The Slanted Sample? Here, our motto is, "You go in with the best intentions, but leave just a little bit skewed." Join our many other waiting customers and test one of our specialty drinks. For example, you may want to select The

Delayed Meeting – one shot of gin, two shots of whiskey, and three hours disappear before you know what has happened. Or try The Scope Creep, a smooth blend of Kahlua, Crème de Menthe, and 151 Rum. You start out thinking you only have time for one, but soon they take up your entire evening. And of course, no night is really complete without enjoying our signature drink, The Slanted Sample. It's not a purely random selection of alcohol; it's whatever we haven't sold lately.

Now your table is ready. Don't worry about being seated near the kitchen. We know you want the opportunity to observe the entire process, so every table is near the kitchen.

A good dinner begins by obtaining a clear understanding of the meal's overall objectives and the resulting opportunities. What better way to gain that initial understanding than with an appetizer? I suggest, for your first experience with us, The Sampletizer – a collection of our four favorite starters. Begin with the Charter Cheese Fries: One bite and they will be your raison d'être. Then move on to the Nacho Access. Others may try to keep them to themselves, but the Charter Cheese Fries will be your ticket in. Some chips left over? Use them to dig into our ERM Eight-layer Dip. The governance is good, but the control activities add the spice. And finally, we present Jalapeño Popper-inners, because just when you don't expect a visit – "pop" – there they are.

Once the appetizers are finished, it is time to closely evaluate what you want your meal to accomplish. In the next course, you have to carefully scrutinize your alternatives, recognize the control you must exert, and weigh the answer to the ultimate question – risk versus reward, or, as it is more commonly phrased, soup or salad?

Salad is the safer alternative. There is nothing inherently risky here. Oh, maybe the occasional spot of dressing on one's shirt or blouse, but overall a salad is a solid alternative that analysis will show to bring its own reward. Yes, salads are safe, but at Chez Auditing we try to do more. We've put a little more teeth into one of the classic salads by adding confidential ingredients that reach out and grab your taste buds, resulting in the Caesar Records Salad. The Chef's Salad includes ham, boiled eggs, and cheese, but will leave you asking for more with the addition of our favorite ICQberg lettuce. And for the truly risk-averse, we offer the Auditee's Answer Salad – lettuce alone.

However, there will be those in your party who want to stretch out, strive for more, and take more risks. These are the individuals who are willing to take their chances with the potential spill of hot liquid, who accept the hazards of the attendant stains and scaldings. These are the bold adventurers who will say, "Soup for me!" If you are willing to accept that risk, you will have the unmitigated opportunity to try our Auditor's Stew, a blend of ingredients that ensures all necessary sources have been included. However, I suggest you reduce the inherent risk and sample our soon-to-be world famous Audit Gazpacho. This unique blend of cool gazpacho with clam chowder results in a dish just as cold and clammy as its name.

So far, the meal has all been preparation – discussions, reviews, inquiry. Now it is time to get to the true heart of the audit/meal experience – the meat, if you will. And one of Chez Auditing's most famous meat dishes is the Nitpicker's Shish-ka-bob, where the meat, fruit, and vegetables are grilled right on the bayonet. Are you more the seafood type? Then you definitely want to try our grilled COSO Salmon. But the entree that will really sneak up on you is the Chicken Cacciafraudie.

End your meal "write" by enjoying our array of "final presentations." If the full meal has been too much for you, you may want to try our collection of light sorbets we call The Clean Finding. On the other hand, maybe you can't get enough – enough chocolate, that is. We "found" every chocolaty thing we could and piled it high in one bowl that we call The Chocolate Tower of Incredibly Picky Issues. And, of course, there is everything in between, from the Two-faced Crème Brulee (sugar-coat it, then blast it with heat) to the Exit Meeting (what else? Rhubarb pie). However, I must warn you that all final presentations may take up to one hour to prepare because management constantly rewrites the recipes.

We thank you for your time and hope you find this blend of discussion, partnership, and analysis exhilarating. Just remember: Chez Auditing is a self-serve operation for, after all, at Chez Auditing we don't do original work.

INTERNAL AUDITING
THE GAME

Congratulations on your purchase of Internal Auditing: The Game. You and three of your friends – or acquaintances who just really want a good audit opinion – are about to embark on a fun-filled experience featuring interviews, spreadsheet creation, reporting, and the various joys and excitement that are internal auditing … and Internal Auditing: The Game. We know you can't wait to get this internal audit started, so let's begin.

Equipment
Before starting, ensure that you have the tools required for a successful game. Your game packet should include: game board, five dice (four-, six-, eight-, 12-, and 20-sided), four mechanical pencils, 50 Findings cards, 16 Auditee cards, 160 Discussion cards, play money, spreadsheets, 11 rule appendices, and four tokens (an IIA five-year pin, an audit charter, an ERM cube, and the Red Book).

If any of these items are missing, conduct a second review to corroborate the results of the initial test. Once confirmation of missing equipment is achieved, prepare a written report of the situation for the owner of the game. The report should include an opinion on the control environment that allowed the piece(s) to go missing, as well as suggested corrective actions. In the event you are the owner, prepare a memo to the Audit Committee describing the potential conflict of interest, as well as your resignation.

Preparation for Play

First determine which player will be the auditor-in-charge (AIC). Accomplish this by playing Senior Executive/Final Report/Auditor. Remember, Senior Executive beats Auditor, Auditor beats Final Report, and Final Report beats Senior Executive.

Once the AIC is selected, the other players will prepare for game play. Unfold the game board. Shuffle the 16 Auditee cards and place them in the various offices on the game board. Shuffle the Findings cards and place them on the main desk in the Audit Department. Shuffle the Discussion cards and place 10 on each of the auditees' offices. Each player will select one mechanical pencil and a token to represent his or her internal auditor. The AIC will then double check to ensure the game has been set up correctly. From this review, the AIC will prepare review notes regarding any errors, discrepancies, or differences of opinion related to setting up the game. Record your review notes on the spreadsheets.

Starting with the AIC, each person rolls the dice to determine the skill level of his or her auditor in the following categories: intelligence, analytical skill, and business knowledge (all positive traits); as well as charisma, compassion, and personality (all negative traits). Record the skill ratings on the spreadsheets.

Game Play

Roll the four-sided die to determine the number of management layers between the Chief Audit Executive and the CEO. If a three or four is rolled, the internal audit shop is considered "ineffective" and the game is over.

Next, starting with the AIC, each person will establish a plan for what he or she will accomplish during the game. The plan should specify how many audits will be completed, how many moves each audit will take, and what metrics will be used to measure the department's success (there must be a minimum of 10). Record the plans on the spreadsheets.

Roll the 12-sided die to determine whether the plan is accepted. If a nine through 12 is rolled, the plan is accepted, the player may continue, and he or she receives the accolades of the Audit Committee along with five experience points. If a five through eight is rolled, the Audit Committee can't quite put its finger on it but something doesn't seem exactly right. Minor modifications are required, and the player must wait one turn before starting the audit plan. The player does not earn any experience points, but does not need to make any changes to the plan. If a one through four is rolled, the Audit Committee gives no explanation but rejects the plan out of hand. The player must rebuild the audit plan from the ground up, earns no experience points, and must present the new plan to the Audit Committee. Remember, if experience points fall below zero, the player is "terminated." Record the experience points on the spreadsheets.

Once the plan is established, players roll the dice to visit various auditees. Use the Discussion cards to determine what occurs in the meeting with those auditees. Discussion cards will generally require reference to the appendices, which include topics such as Fraud Investigation, Bribery, or Report to Human Resources. At the audit's conclusion, roll one die to determine how many Findings cards to draw. If any one of the Findings cards indicates an "effective" audit opinion, all other findings can be ignored. Record the findings on the spreadsheets.

Once the audit process is complete, use the Exit Interview appendix to cross reference the findings, the auditee's temperament, the auditor's skill sets, and the layers between the CAE and CEO to determine the success or failure of the audit. Record the results of the exit interview on the spreadsheets.

Use of Money

The supplied play money represents the bank account for a local IIA chapter. Players will take turns acting as the chapter's Treasurer. When it is time for Treasurer duties to transfer, the player currently acting as Treasurer turns over all cash and documentation to the newly appointed Treasurer. The new Treasurer will verify all cash is on hand, prepare a new budget, and complete all necessary documentation. While acting as Treasurer, the time available for the player to complete audit work will be reduced by half.

Winning the Game

The game ends when one of the following situations occurs:

1. One player completes the audit plan within the planned number of moves.

2. One player achieves all established measures of success.

3. All other auditors get terminated for lack of experience points or promoted to other departments, leaving one player as the only auditor in the company.

4. The C-suite Collusion card is drawn. In this situation, all players must complete a résumé and construct a job search plan. Record this information on the spreadsheets.

Happy Auditing. We hope you enjoy playing Internal Auditing: The Game. Please watch for our upcoming titles Governmental Auditing (all the excitement of Internal Auditing: The Game with the additional break-neck speed of government bureaucracies) and Operational Auditing (walk the fine line between auditing and consulting without jeopardizing your independence and integrity). We are always on the lookout for new titles. If you have a game you think would be a perfect addition to our Internal Audit series, record it on the spreadsheets.

Warning Labels for Internal Audits

In this increasingly litigious world, everyone faces the growing risk of lawsuits. And there is no magic charm which makes internal auditors exempt. As so many others have learned, one of the best defenses is to warn people of the potential limitations and hazards. With that in mind, what follows is a collection of warning labels to be used on internal audit reports.

Controls in hindsight may be less impactful than they appear

Read, lather, repeat

May cause blurriness, trepidation, fatigue, or termination

Do not operate heavy machinery after implementing recommendations

Caution: Findings may have shifted after your agreement

This product not intended to replace real thought

Keep out of reach of childlike minds

Concepts within this report may constitute a choking hazard

Not for human consumption

Warning – reading may cause drowsiness

Do not reuse recommendations for subsequent audits

This product not intended for use as a risk management tool

Keep away from executives

Do not read with blades or sharp implements nearby

Not dishwasher safe

Flammable if handled by irate personalities

IIA headquarters has issued the following press release:

The IIA has always taken a proactive and innovative role in educating auditors and the public on the value of internal audit services. Today, The Institute takes a bold, new step in that direction by announcing it will become a major player in the world of theme-based amusement parks. Secret negotiations conducted over the past two years have resulted in The IIA's acquisition of more than 50,000 acres near its Orlando-area headquarters and the subsequent development of AuditLand – home of the happiest review on earth. Blending state-of-the-art attractions with cutting-edge audit concepts, AuditLand creates an immersive, customer-focused universe of audit experiences that will delight adults and children of all ages.

TAKE A TOUR

After passing through the adequately controlled entrance to AuditLand, guests begin their journey at Main Street Auditing. A re-creation of a turn-of-the-century business district, Main Street Auditing revisits a simpler time – a gentle era when auditors had only to tic, tie, and cross-foot to do their jobs. Everybody will want to join the fun by making their first stop The Spreadsheets of Wonder Pavilion. Here the whole family can work together to diligently inspect page upon page of handwritten spreadsheets in an attempt to determine why the final balance is off by a full dollar.

At the end of Main Street is Compliance Hub. From there, paths branch off in five directions, leading to the park's separate themed areas. Each is closely linked to the world of internal auditing and jam-packed with thrilling, experience-based attractions.

LET THE ADVENTURE BEGIN

Auditing AdventureLand showcases the perils and pitfalls that internal auditors face every day. Whether you take the harrowing journey through Paper Cut Tree House, dodge the threats of the Enchanted Outsourcing Room, or get stuck in Indiana Jones and the Airport of Cancelled Flights, you'll love the thrills of this wondrous land.

Auditing AdventureLand's premiere attraction is the Control Jungle Cruise, where guests can enjoy an up-close look at the jungle of an uncontrolled environment. Immediately after leaving the dock, the riverboat plunges into the darkness of wild growth. In the distance, a group of accountants dance and holler as they blatantly complete their work with no separation of duties. Then, a tribe of supervisors signs expense reports without looking at the associated support. Finally, a rampaging senior vice president attacks the riverboat, forcing the captain to fire off his trusty audit charter. The vice president, realizing his defeat, quickly turns tail and runs. Guests then arrive back at the dock, having survived the horrors of an uncontrolled environment.

STAYING IN CONTROL

The audit adventure continues in ControlLand – an environment where resources are never an issue and everything is perfectly controlled. The area's perimeter is surrounded by barbed wire, an electric fence, attack dogs, and guards with really bad attitudes. ControlLand has only one entrance. And once guests leave, they'll need more than a hand stamp to get back in. The passwords administered upon entering must be changed every hour.

Of course, anyone who hasn't changed his or her password will get the opportunity to ride The Help Desk, an amazing re-creation of the technical support experience. "Your visit is very important to us. We are experiencing heavier than normal volume. Please remain in line and our next representative will assist you shortly. If you would like to visit us on the Web, feel free to return home and log on to www.sellyoursoulforanID.com."

Nestled deep within ControlLand is the spookiest ride in all of AuditLand – the Audit Mansion. From the outside, all appears well in this 19th century-style dwelling. But the minute guests walk into the first musty room, littered with eraser shavings and paper dust, they'll find themselves in the presence of unearthly audit forces. Walking through the hallways of this sinister mansion, visitors will have the feeling of being observed. No one will be able to see who the examiners are, however, until they've reached the mansion's central room. As the room stretches – yes, stretches – the lights grow stronger, revealing a group of elderly individuals overhead wearing green eyeshades and holding spreadsheets and pencils. Visitors suddenly realize this is no normal house – they're trapped inside the Auditing Retirement Home. The guests are then quickly whisked away in their own personal wheelchairs to visit the retired auditors' various haunts, including the Room of Eternal Exit Interviews, the Constantly Flowing Flowcharts, the Banquet of Rubber Chicken, and the Attic of Unfunctional Functional Tests. At the ride's conclusion, a distant voice cries, "We are the home of 999 happy retired auditors. But there's always room for one more."

DISCOVER THE WORLD OF FRAUD
Fraudland, the park's third main area, appeals to the larcenist in each of us. Children especially will enjoy FraudLand's gentle dark rides, including Peter Ponzi's Flight, Mr. Kozlowski's Wild Ride, and The Many Adventures of Winnie the Tax Evader.

The global impact of fraud truly comes to life in It's a Global Audit World. Riding in small boats, visitors float from country to country while small dolls representing auditors throughout the world raise their pencils in salute as they count inventory, interrogate clients, and input data. Global Audit World's enchanting theme song plays throughout the entire ride:

> *"It's a world of findings that slip through holes.*
> *It's a world of errors and a lack of controls.*
> *There's so much that goes wrong with the frauds and the cons.*
> *It's a global problem after all."*

AUDITING RUN AMUCK

ConsultantLand is a place where normal audit practices are ignored and the customer is king. It's the home of Honey, I CSA'd the Audience, a 3-D film that makes guests feel like they're right in the middle of a self-assessment, and Auditopia, a ride that lets everyone drive their own little audit program around the audit universe – just remember, no bumping and no scope creep.

The theater-in-the-round concept is turned upside down with the Carousel of Audits – the centerpiece of Consultantland. In this show house, the audience revolves around the stage, instead of vice versa. The performance begins with a reenactment of the history of auditing from the dawn of time. Cavemen make stone tools, grind corn, and discover fire, while the prehistoric auditors look over their shoulders to ensure flint chip counts, kernel usage, and exposure to heat are all appropriately recorded and controlled. Each subsequent scene then reveals the gradual evolution of auditors into consultants. The performance concludes with a depiction of auditing's future, where all people are auditors and everyone can control themselves.

STEP ABOARD THE ENTERPRISE

After experiencing the joys of consulting, even risk-averse guests will want to visit ERM World, AuditLand's most enterprising area. For audit thrill-seekers, ERM World offers the high-speed adventures of Sarbox Mountain. From the start of their journey, riders feel a sense of disorientation as they twist and turn through the lightless void. Then, the attraction reveals a glimmer of hope as light becomes visible at the ride's summit. This hope proves false, however, as the coaster then plunges back into the darkness. Along the way, irate audit clients appear from dark corners, attempting to snatch the riders from successfully completing their journey. Upon their return to the station, guests will have experienced the heights and depths of Sarbox Mountain.

ERM World also features a unique seafaring experience – Auditors of the Caribbean. What starts as a pleasant boat trip through a quiet audit shop takes an unexpected turn as guests head down a deserted passageway. A disembodied voice begins to explain that the company may have problems with offshore entities. Suddenly, the boat slides down the slippery embankment that leads to offshore corporations. Guests will feel as if they've been transported to a small Caribbean island as they sail past lifelike re-creations of auditors raiding an offshore company to discover where the profits have really gone. The auditors break into a room where some nefarious scheme is being hatched. Bankers in tailor-made three-piece suits appear to be jumping out the windows as auditors in off-the-rack bargain attire break the doors down with their computers in hand. In another scene, a banker sits with a scrub bucket and dollar bills attached to a line of rope. Yes, the auditors have discovered a money-laundering scheme. Next, the auditors are seen selling off the assets of the closed company to the highest bidders. At the ride's conclusion, the chief executive officer proclaims the auditors heroes as they give a 21-slide PowerPoint presentation demonstrating their accomplishments.

GIFTS, DINING, AND EVENING ENTERTAINMENT

Of course, there's more to AuditLand than just rides. The park features many exciting specialty shops, including Great Cover-ups (a hat store), Fudging the Books (a combination candy and book store), Timely Processing (a watch store), and Inappropriate Gifts and Gratuities – the largest gift shop in AuditLand. After working up an appetite, guests can enjoy fine cuisine at several eateries, including Cold Hard Facts (ice cream), Hot Cross-referenced Buns (bakery), Braut and Paid For (German food), Caught Redhanded (seafood), and Effective and Efficient (fast food). Also, kids will enjoy the meet-and-greet areas, where they can visit all their favorite characters, including Arnie the Auditing Aardvark, Freddie Fraudster, Controller Cat, and the most popular of all, Sammie the Self-assessing Sea Serpent.

Once the sun begins to set on AuditLand, the park gears up for an evening of excitement guests will never forget. The fun begins with the parade of Auditing Stars – a full mile of men and women in business suits marching to the stirring strains of the Audit Club March. The AuditLand experience then concludes with an impressive display of fireworks – a half-hour of IIA branded blue and white pyrotechnics synchronized with the song, "An Audit Is a Wish Your Audit Committee Makes."

THE WONDERFUL WORLD OF AUDIT

Pack up the kids, spend the day, and experience what every auditor already knows – AuditLand is like nothing you've ever observed. Once you've been there, you'll want to follow up again and again and again.

A PITCH SESSION at the New Audit Cable Network

WRITER: "Cartoons. That's the way you make this network a success. Cartoons about internal auditors."

EXECUTIVE: "You've got to be kidding …"

WRITER: "No. Hear me out on this. Kids love cartoons. They watch cartoons. If those cartoons are about internal auditors, then they want to grow up to be internal auditors. Humor, kids, pratfalls, internal auditors – it just reeks of success!"

EXECUTIVE: "You're wasting my time, get out of …"

WRITER: "I'm not taking 'no' for an answer. Here's a surefire winner; a cartoon every kid will love. There's a group of teenagers who go around in a van performing audits – Freddy the CAE, Daphne the staff auditor, Velma the CAATs expert, and Baggy the disheveled investigator who gets everyone fired. But the real star is their Great Dane – Scooby Don't. Whenever the auditees try to come up with some excuse for poor controls, he barks out his catch phrase: 'Rooby Rooby Ron't.' Every episode will end with the audit client saying, 'And I would've gotten away with the inefficiency if it hadn't been for those meddling auditors.'"

EXECUTIVE: "Meh."

WRITER: "Fine. This one'll knock your socks off! Because everyone is interested in the future of auditing, we can do a cartoon about a family of auditors in the year 2525. As futuristic auditors, they perform consulting services. But there's a twist: Their consulting practice focuses on downsizing operations. They're called the Jettisons and there's George, Jane his wife, daughter Judy, their boy Elroy, and their dog Justgo."

EXECUTIVE: "You've got a thing about dogs, don't you?"

WRITER: "Dogs are funny."

EXECUTIVE: "No, they aren't."

WRITER: "Well, then – no dogs in this one – but lots of animals. This one is called George of the Judgment. George is an auditor who was raised by a jungle-based external audit team of giant apes. He's got an elephant named Schlep who does all the legwork for him, and he travels to the deepest, darkest jungles to pass judgment on his clients. As he swings from vine to vine you can hear the clients yelling to each other, 'Watch out for that fee!'"

EXECUTIVE: "That's not internal auditing."

WRITER: "I was hoping you wouldn't notice. Okay, okay, I'm not beat yet. Here's one that's so good I won't even have to give you the synopsis. I can sell you on it with just the theme song. Listen:

> *Who works on an audit test under the sea?*
> *SpreadBob SheetPants!*
> *Repellent and mellow and boring is he.*
> *SpreadBob SheetPants!*
> *If auditor nonsense be something you need.*
> *SpreadBob SheetPants!*
> *Then pull out your bayonets, make them all bleed.*
> *SpreadBob SheetPants!*"

EXECUTIVE: "You've got to be kidding."

WRITER: "Well, then instead of a cartoon, we could film a live series called The Bad Audit Splits. There will be four big fluffy audit characters – Fleagle who runs away from every confrontation, Bingo who agrees with every audit client, Drooper who mopes around sadly accepting his role as an audit lifer, and Snork who can only honk his elephant nose but is in charge of oral presentations. They drive from audit site to audit site in little audit dune buggies singing this song:

> *One bad audit, two bad audits, three bad audits, four...*
> *Four bad audits make a plan and so do many more.*
> *Running from the findings the Bad Audit Buggies go.*
> *If everything's effective it's much easier you know.*
> *Tra-la-la, la la la la, Tra-la-la, la ..."*

EXECUTIVE: "Stop singing!"

WRITER: "You're not a fan of songs or my singing. Got it. I've tossed you some of my best ideas, but I've still got a lot of really great ones. How about an audit clerk named Audit Clerk who works with Audit Report Specialist Polly Puredread. Unfortunately, Polly lives in dread of having to report any findings. Whenever she thinks she is going to have to face the client with bad news, she begins singing, 'Oh where, oh where has my Thunderdog gone?' Unknown to her, humble, lovable Audit Clerk turns into her savior Thunderdog who, with the phrase 'There's no need to be yellow, Thunderdog will bellow,' yells and blusters until the audit client is willing to accept anything in the audit report whether it's true or not. His arch nemeses include Simon Bar Sycophant, who spends all his time sucking up to the CAE, and Rift Wrath who ..."

EXECUTIVE: "NO DOGS!"

WRITER: "Sheesh, that's right – no dogs, no songs. Okay, let me just throw out some quick thoughts. A CAE mixes 'dibs and dabs of everything drab' along with Chemical Xternal to build an audit team called the Powerless Puff Auditors. Or, Mr. McClueless. He's a shortsighted auditor who thinks he understands the way things work. But he is so focused on internal measurements within his own department he completely ignores what the audit client needs. Or a Mounted Auditor named Dudley Do-Risk who is in charge of the department's audit planning. He works for Inspector FindRisk, is in love with the Inspector's daughter Quell, and they are constantly battling against Slightly Shortcash."

EXECUTIVE: "No, no, and no."

WRITER: "Oh, brother. All right, not the best on my list, but let's try these. Auditing Guy, about an auditor and his irreverent family where the plot always takes a back seat to the auditing non sequiturs and flashbacks with phrases like 'I haven't seen a dinner like this since my kickback from Bernie Madoff.' Or another family-oriented cartoon called The Simpletons. The father is the auditor at a nuclear power plant where he spends his time counting donuts. Or a flying superhero named Micromanaging Mouse who leaps into action with the cry, 'Here I come to tic and tie.'"

EXECUTIVE: "Never, never, and never."

WRITER: "I'm getting to the end of my list. Here are some titles. Cocky and Hoodwinkle? Quickdraw McGraudit? Sarbanes-Oxley's Home for Imaginary Controls?"

EXECUTIVE: "I have no idea what you're talking about."

WRITER: "What's wrong? How can you not like these ideas? These are hilarious."

EXECUTIVE: "Look, son. I know you're excited and you really think these are great. But let me let you in on a little secret … auditors just aren't funny."

REQUEST FOR ★ URGENT ★ BUSINESS RELATIONSHIP!

First, I must solicit your strictest confidence in this transaction. This is by virtue of its nature as being utterly confidential and "top secret." I am sure and have confidence in your ability and reliability, as an auditor, to complete a transaction of this great magnitude involving a pending transaction requiring maximum confidentiality.

We are top officials of a government contract review panel who are interested in completion of audits within our country. However, our audit findings are presently trapped in a small country. In order to complete our audits, we solicit your assistance in transferring into your account the said trapped findings.

The source of these findings are as follows: During the last military regime within the small country, the government officials set up companies and audited themselves in a way that over-controlled various ministries. The present civilian government set up a contract review panel, and we have identified a lot of inflated contract findings which are presently floating in the central audit department of the small country ready for solutions.

However, by virtue of our position as civil servants and members of this panel, we cannot report these findings in our names. I have therefore been delegated as a matter of trust by my colleagues of the panel to look for an overseas partner into whose reports we would transfer the findings, totaling a number that would ensure meeting all key performance measures and balanced scorecard results. Hence we are writing you this letter. We have agreed to share the findings thus: 20% for the account owner (you), 70% for us (the officials), and 10% to be used in separate reports related to taxation and local and foreign expenses.

Please note that this transaction is 100% safe, and we hope to commence the transfer at the latest seven (7) banking days from the date of the receipt of the following information by fax: your company's signed and stamped letterhead, a list of your current findings, and access to your electronic workpapers. This way we will use your company's name to apply for the findings and re-award the findings as agreed.

We are looking forward to doing this business with you and solicit your confidentiality in this transaction. I will send you detailed information of this pending project when I have heard from you.

Yours faithfully,

Dr. Euell Rudy Day

Do You Take This Auditor?

The IIA is proud to announce its latest value-added service – "Internal Audit Themed Weddings." Yes, you can now bring together two of life's greatest experiences – the union of two people and a strong control environment – in one spectacular event.

Internal Audit Themed Weddings are where the elements of a traditional audit are blended with effective and efficient nuptials, allowing the happy couple to share with friends and families their love for each other and their love for internal auditing.

Of course, the success of any wedding – as with any audit – takes extensive planning. For an Internal Audit Themed Wedding, that planning begins by considering the objectives of the wedding. Once all parties agree to those objectives, the couple begins identifying significant risks associated with the wedding. (In the spirit of full disclosure, we want to note that our initial testing included the subsequent marriage in that risk assessment. However, our sample indicated this resulted in an inordinate number of couples changing their plans and declining marriage to join nunneries, monasteries, etc. As part of our corrective action we have limited the scope of the risk assessment to just the wedding itself.) Finally, an initial assessment of the adequacy and effectiveness of the couple's control is determined. Opportunities for improvement in these areas can be included in the wedding ceremony.

Once the planning is over, it is time to go into the field and have a wedding. With our top package, the proceedings occur in a perfect replica of the boardroom and, for an extra fee, the wedding can actually occur during an audit committee meeting. Guests enter and sign the guest register, which is published by The IIA Bookstore. (Copies are available at the end of the ceremony, with a 20 percent discount available for IIA members.)

The groomsmen (dressed in traditional dark suits) enter with the groom (dressed in a matching white suit). All comb-overs are perfectly aligned. The processional starts, and the bridesmaids make their entrance wearing business suits that have been designed to match the groomsmen's perfectly. Their glasses have been polished to gleaming perfection and their hair is coiffed in tight buns. Of course, the maid of honor will have the tallest bun of all. (Some of our packages allow for business casual. However, the couple should be aware of the risk they are accepting related to the professionalism of the ceremony.)

Then it is time for the most important part of the processional. And what bride wouldn't look radiant walking down the aisle to the strains of "Here Comes the Bride (based on substantive testing that indicates controls are adequate to ensure she is, indeed, the bride)"? The crowd will smile, sigh, and weep when they see her bedecked in a business suit of white and holding a bouquet of red and yellow books. For our standard wedding, the ceremony will be presided over by the most recent winner of the Bradford Cadmus Award.

The ceremony starts with the background, laying out the history of the happy couple. Then the scope of the marriage is explained, including scope limitations (for example, 'til issuance of the final report do you part). At this point, the couple will exchange test findings as a token of their shared conclusions. Each is then asked, "Do you take this auditor to be your lawfully wedded husband/wife, providing reasonable assurance that you will love and cherish, have and hold, and tic and tie – forsaking all other audit shops – for as long as you both have previously agreed to during your engagement

notifications?"
(Alternate ICQs are
available upon request.)

Upon acceptance of the
conclusions drawn from
this interview, and
assuming there be
no audit committee
member present who
objects to the final
opinion, the happy
couple will hear
these words: "By
the power given
unto me by The IIA
and by the laws of
the state of Florida,
I now pronounce you,
effectively, husband and
wife! In my opinion,
the control structure related to this wedding is sufficient to ensure
achievement of its objectives, including your ability to kiss the bride.
Whom the Standards have determined to be in compliance, let no
subsequent findings result in an ineffective report. I now present to you as
husband and wife and co-auditors-in-charge, Mr. and Mrs. Smith."

And with those words, the newly bound couple will head back up the aisle
as the guests shower them with shredded copies of old Internal Auditor
magazines. Awaiting them will be even more of the joys and benefits of The
IIA's Internal Audit Themed Weddings. But we are running out of time and
space. You'll just have to contact us to learn about such choices as the available
documentary evidence (photographs, video, or written report), theme for
your reception (the classic COSO, the somewhat outdated but still popular
Sarbanes-Oxley, or the edgy GRC), or location for your honeymoon (IIA
headquarters, the Auditor's Hall of Fame, or the incredibly popular Auditland).
In conclusion, let us share some of the customer survey results from
happy couples who have experienced the testing phase of Internal Audit

Themed Weddings:

"I've never felt such assurance in any celebration."

"Everything was under perfect control."

"It was the separate quality assurance process that gave me security."

"Condition, cause, criteria, effect, corrective action – it had everything. Who could want more?"

Yes, it can all be yours – the glamour, the splendor, and the unadulterated objectivity of an Internal Audit Themed Wedding. (And don't forget, with an additional generous donation to The IIA Research Foundation, you will also receive a wedding brick that will be part of our newly planned wedding pavilion.)

Casablanca

ALMOST THE GREATEST AUDIT MOVIE EVER MADE

In a startling discovery, researchers working at the Warner Brothers archives have found the first draft of the script for the classic movie Casablanca. In this original version, Humphrey Bogart plays Rick Blaine as a disaffected chief audit executive for Casablanca Inc.; a career auditor whose only desire is to keep his head down long enough to reach retirement with full pension. His department (affectionately known as Rick's Audit Shop) is not necessarily an honest audit shop, but it is the one place of refuge where anyone can get a job and hide.

Into the department walks Rick's former co-worker, Ilsa Lund, with her new manager, Victor Laszlo. Ilsa and Victor still believe internal audit shops can make a difference. They have come to Casablanca as part of a benchmarking project. But, in the passions of a late-night workpaper review, Ilsa rekindles something in Rick he thought he had lost long ago — a belief in what internal auditing can really mean to a company.

Being fortunate enough to obtain access to that original script, we present some of the most famous quotes, as they would have been spoken had this version been produced.

CAPT. RENAULT: Major Strasser has been defrauded. Round up the usual suspects.

RICK: Don't you sometimes wonder if it's worth all this? I mean all that ticking and tying?

VICTOR: You might as well question why we breathe. If we stop breathing, we'll die. If we stop testing the financial statements, the company will die.

RICK: Well, what of it? It would be out of its misery.

VICTOR: You know how you sound, Mr. Blaine? Like a man who's trying to convince himself of something he hasn't found the evidence to support.

ILSA: Play it once, Sam. For old times sake.

SAM: [lying] I don't know what you mean, Miss Ilsa.

ILSA: Play it, Sam. Play "As Deadlines Go By."

SAM: [lying] Oh, I can't remember it, Miss Ilsa. I'm a little rusty on it.

ILSA: I'll hum it for you. Da-dy-da-dy-dadum, da-dy-da-dee-da-dum...
[Sam begins playing.]

ILSA: Sing it, Sam.

SAM: [singing] You must remember this/A list is just a list/A test is just a test/The auditees will all resist/Deadlines go by/And when the audit's due/There's always work to do/Or you must do one more review/No matter what the findings bring...

RICK: [rushing up] Sam, I thought I told you never to play...
[Sees Ilsa. Sam closes his laptop and walks away.]

CAPT. RENAULT: This is the end of the benchmarking.

RICK: Twenty bucks says it isn't.

CAPT. RENAULT: Is that a serious offer?

RICK: I just paid out 20. I'd like to get it back.

CAPT. RENAULT: Make it 10. I'm only a poor corrupt executive.

MAJ. STRASSER: We have a complete Human Resources file on you. Richard Blaine, internal auditor, age 57. Cannot work for any other company. The reason is a little vague. We also know what you did in the Paris casino in Las Vegas, Mr. Blaine, and why you had to leave. [hands the file to Rick] Don't worry, we are not going to forward it.

RICK: [reading] Am I really a mid to low contributor?

[Talking about Rick.]

MAJ. STRASSER: You give him credit for too much cleverness. My impression was that he's just another blundering auditor.

CAPT. RENAULT: We mustn't underestimate "blundering auditors." I was with them when they "blundered" into WorldCom years ago.

RICK: Of all the audit shops, in all the companies, in all the world, she benchmarks mine.

CAPT. RENAULT: What in heaven's name brought you to Casablanca?

RICK: Creativity. I came to Casablanca for the creativity.

CAPT. RENAULT: The creativity? What creativity? You're in internal auditing.

RICK: I was misinformed.

CAPT. RENAULT: Have you lost your mind?

RICK: I have. Sit down!

CAPT. RENAULT: Put that report down!

RICK: I don't want to issue it, but I will if you take one more step!

CAPT. RENAULT: [amused] Under the circumstances I will sit down.

RICK: Last night we reviewed a great many things. You said I was to do the analysis for both of us. Well, I've done a lot of analyzing since then, and it all adds up to one thing: You're getting on that plane with Victor to consult with a new company.

ILSA: But, Richard, no, I... I...

RICK: Now, you've got to listen to me! You have any idea what you'd have to look forward to if you stayed here? Nine chances out of 10, we'd both wind up in accounting. Isn't that true, Louie?

CAPT. RENAULT: I'm afraid the CEO would insist.

ILSA: You're only saying this to make me leave.

RICK: I'm saying it because it's true. We both know you belong with

Victor. You're part of his benchmarking team, the one thing that keeps that team together. If that plane leaves the ground and you're not with him, you'll regret it. Maybe not today. Maybe not tomorrow. But soon and for the rest of your career.

ILSA: But what about us?

RICK: We'll always have the International Conference. We didn't have… we … we lost it until you came to Casablanca. We got it back last night.

ILSA: I said I would never work for anyone else again.

RICK: And you never will. But I've got a job to do, too. Where I'm auditing, you can't do follow-up. What I've got to review, you can't be any part of. Ilsa, I'm no good at being objective, but it doesn't take much to see that the careers of three little people don't amount to a hill of beans in this crazy company. Someday you'll understand that. [Ilsa lowers her head and begins to cry.]

RICK: Now, now… [Rick gently places his hand under her chin and raises it so their eyes meet.] Here's auditing you, kid.

And that final, classic line that even a change of subject couldn't change:

RICK: Louis, I think this is the beginning of a beautiful friendship.

the most INTERESTING AUDITOR *in the* WORLD

If he were to get a fact wrong, it would still be correct

The audit committee meets in his office

He gets e-mails with potential findings… from other companies

His computer battery never dies

IT holds conferences about him

His executive summaries never exceed one page

He found the control breakdown that allowed people to mess with Texas

He has done original work

He once perfectly balanced risk and control

His tick marks are self-explanatory

He went to the chief risk officer… to warn him

He has memorized his IIA member number

His meetings always end five minutes early

He has never received a review note

For him, business casual is a two-piece suit

He has removed the delete key from his computer

He once got marketing to establish effective controls

He teaches old auditors new tricks

He adds value by just looking at a department

He bandages the wounded

He is...The Most Interesting Auditor in the World

> *"I don't always conduct audits, but when I do, I follow the IIA Standards. Stay inquisitive my friends."*

ALICE IN AUDITLAND

It all started quietly enough for Alice as she sat in the company's reception lounge reading the corporate newsletter, waiting to be admitted into Human Resources. She was quite bored (for after all, the newsletter had few pictures, and the pictures it did have were out of focus) so she was delighted to see a Corporate Auditor come running through the lobby. Her delight turned to curiosity as the auditor cried, "Oh, dear! Oh, dear! I shall be late" and took a timekeeping slip and a pencil out of his waistcoat pocket to record his time. Her curiosity was a natural curiosity that arose from the opportunity to actually see such the rare creature in its natural habitat. Why was he using something as ancient as a pencil? Why was he running late? Where could he be going?" She found herself so entranced by the auditor that she began to follow him and, in short order, found herself falling, falling, falling down into the Audit Hole.

The fall took a very long time and Alice had ample opportunity to understand the errors of her ways because, while Alice may not have known much, she did know that falling this deeply into an Audit Hole could not be good for her career. But, the voyage was long enough that she also had time to come to grips with her misfortune. "I shall just have to take control of myself," she thought. It was at that exact moment she reached the bottom of the hole.

She was not hurt, for she had landed in what she assumed was a large lake. But one taste of the water was enough to make her quickly realize she had actually landed in a pool of tears. "What," she wondered, "could cause so many tears?" She listened closely and realized she was hearing a quiet sobbing. "Although I have fallen for an awfully long time and have dropped into this pool, I am quite sure it is not me who is crying," she said to herself. She continued to listen intently. As her eyes became accustomed to the light and as her ears became accustomed to the sounds, she recognized the source of the sobbing. She realized she was in a pool of auditees' tears.

She swam to the edge of the pool and climbed out next to the group of auditees. "Well, we must pull ourselves together," said one auditee, and the sobbing stopped. "All this crying seems to have made us all exceedingly damp, and I am not sure how we will get dry again."

"I have an idea," the mousiest auditee said. "Please, all sit down and listen" and, once they were all seated, the mousy auditee began to read. "The objective of this audit is to ensure that the policies, processes, and procedures in place are sufficient to…"

"What are you doing?" Alice asked.

"Why, the driest things I know of are audit reports," answered the mousy auditee and continued to read aloud.

The highest ranking auditee, a Director of Strategic Direction, finally interrupted. "This will never work. I have a much better strategy. Let us have a race. And, when the race is over, we will all be dry." They asked how they should start and the Director said, "However, you would like." They asked where they should race and the Director said, "Anywhere you would like." So they all took off running; bouncing and careening off each other as absolute chaos reigned.

After running around for a short time, Alice approached the Director. "Who is in charge?"

He turned to her, seemingly delighted with the carnage occurring around him. "Isn't it obvious? I am."

"Well, then," Alice asked, "Shouldn't you be stepping in to regain some control?"

"Of course not," answered the Director. "They have all been empowered. They are all one team and, together, we can get much more done if everyone takes responsibility for their own tasks."

Alice looked out across the pandemonium. "It doesn't appear that much is being accomplished."

"Of course it is," said the Director. "Just look at all that activity."

Alice was not convinced. "But, there are quite a large number of people. Are you sure you don't need any help overseeing this…progress?"

The Director looked perturbed. "Of course not!"

At that moment, an assistant to the Director slipped over to Alice and whispered in her ear. "They are all paid the same amount. If there was anyone else in charge, we would have to pay them more."

Alice, realizing she was now dry, decided it was best to move on and quietly slipped away.

She had gone no small distance when she turned a corner and stumbled across a great, large Auditor who was sitting on a very high chair. He peered down at Alice over a long sheet he held. (Alice peeked and saw the letters "I", "C", and "Q.")

"Who are you?" The Auditor asked.

"I am Alice," Alice answered.

The Auditor wrote a note. "Why are you here?"

"I would be happy to tell you," answered Alice, "but I don't really know myself."

The Auditor looked down at her. "If you do not know yourself, how do you know you are Alice?"

Alice pondered this for a while and decided it best to change the subject. "Is that question on your list?"

"You misunderstand," said the Auditor. "I am the Auditor. I do not have to explain myself. I ask the questions. And, because you do not seem to know yourself, I ask again…who are you?"

Alice stood straight and tall. "I am Alice."

"There still seems to be some question of that," the Auditor said with a disgusted smirk, "But let us go on. What are you doing here?"

Exasperated, Alice answered, "As I have said, I do not know. In fact, I was sorely hoping you might be able to provide me the answer to that very question."

The Auditor pulled himself to his full (seated) height. "Believe me. I know what you should be doing. But I cannot tell you what you should be doing. That would mean my questions had no meaning. I can only try to determine what you think you are doing. What is it you think you are doing?"

Alice, still confused, summoned her best response. "Well, I guess you could say that what I am doing is following a corporate auditor who ran past me into these hallways and I was trying to determine what he was doing."

"It is not your job to find out what people are doing, that is my job," the Auditor shouted. "The Audit Charter is very clear on this and you are not to infringe on my review, and never forget that I have the unqualified right to ask these questions and you must answer them…" and the Auditor went on and on.

"I am not sure who or what this person is," Alice thought. "However, I am quite sure that he knows even less than I." And so, she left to see if she could find some other way out.

Turning at the first hallway she spied, Alice saw a large meeting room titled "Boardroom." She entered and almost tripped over a great table with many seats. Cramped at one end were three Executives – a Mr. Hare, a Mr. Hatter, and a Mr. Dormouse. Mr. Dormouse was fast asleep, and the other two were using him as a cushion. Tired from her travels, Alice began to sit down, but Mr. Hare and Mr. Hatter jumped up screaming "No room! No room! We don't need anyone else. We don't need your input. There's no room." Mr. Dormouse continued to sleep.

"Why, there's plenty of room," countered Alice as she tried to sit again.

"No, there isn't. And you can't sit there," Mr. Hare said. "That is the chair that is to be used by the Chair of the Audit Committee."

"And who might the Chair of the Audit Committee be?" asked Alice.

"I am," answered Mr. Hare.

"Then, why are you not sitting here?"

"Because," answered Mr. Hare, "I am also on the Compensation Committee, and my chair is here."

Alice shook her head as she tried to understand. She moved to the next seat. "No! You can't sit at that chair!" shouted Mr. Hare. "That is the chair that is to be used by the Chair of the Compensation Committee."

Exasperated, Alice asked, "And, are you also the Chair of the Compensation Committee?"

Mr. Hare appeared shocked and upset. "Of course not. That would not be proper." Mr. Hare pointed to Mr. Hatter, "he is." Mr. Hatter, though not having said much of anything to this point, sat up more proudly.

"Then," continued Alice, "why is he not sitting in this chair?"

"Because the Board of Directors is currently meeting, and he is a member of the board. The Board of Director chairs are here."

"And I suppose," Alice said, pointing to another seat, "That I can't sit there, either."

"Why, of course not," said Mr. Hare. "That is the chair that is to be used by the Chair of the Board of Directors."

"And are you or Mr. Hatter that Chair?" asked Alice.

Now, Mr. Hare looked even more hurt. "That would be truly wrong. Neither one of us is. Rather, it is he," and both Mr. Hare and Mr. Hatter pointed to the sleeping Mr. Dormouse. "But, do not disturb him; he is contemplating decisions that have been forwarded from the Chairs of the Compensation and Audit Committees."

Suddenly, Mr. Hatter jumped up. "I demand a clean slate. Let's all move one place on." He slid over as he spoke, shaking Mr. Dormouse from his slumbers. Mr. Dormouse moved to the chair formally held by Mr. Hatter. Mr. Hare then moved to Mr. Dormouse's chair.

"Why, what good did that do?" asked Alice.

"It is quite simple," replied Mr. Hare, "now we do not have to worry about the mess we left at our last chair."

Alice thought hard about this. "But doesn't that only mean that the next person will get the mess?"

"Not really," answered Mr. Hare. "They will soon move to a new chair."

Alice was still not sure she understood how anyone would benefit. "Eventually, will you not have to come back to your original mess?"

Mr. Hare looked surprised. "Of course not. By the time I come back around, it is someone else's mess and I don't have to worry."

Alice shook her head in confusion and thought it best to change the subject. "Tell me, why are you all in this board room?"

Mr. Hatter suddenly brightened. "We are working on a very special project for the Chief." Alice noticed that Mr. Hare did not look as excited. "The entire group here," and with that phrase, Mr. Hare swept his arm across the entire table, as if it were full, "felt that, as board members who should be setting an example, it was our job to help the company reduce expenses. Accordingly, we proposed that all employees be required to use approved travel arrangements that we had negotiated. When we presented our information to the Chief, he expressed concern because some of the negotiated rates appeared higher than those that were already being paid."

"That would seem to, indeed, be a problem," Alice said.

"Ah, that just goes to show that, much like the chief, you cannot see the true big picture. Mr. Hatter pointed to the top of a ream of worksheets. "Look here," you can see that the negotiated rate is fifty dollars more than we used to pay. However, I am convinced that we will make up that difference over time."

Alice, not wanting to look too unknowledgeable, studied the paper closely.

Mr. Hatter continued, "We are in the process of proving that I am correct; that, eventually, the difference in costs will be made up for in volume; that, some day, we will hit a point where the negotiated rates are cheaper."

At this point, Mr. Hare leaned over to Alice. "I don't want to say this too loudly because I am sure it will set him off again, but I fear the project is making Mr. Hatter just a little mad. Ever since we started, all he wants to do is change chairs." At that exact moment, Mr. Hatter yelled out. "It is time to move one place. Move on. Move on." Alice decided it was best to just move out of the boardroom.

As she walked down the hallway, Alice felt that she must indeed be getting somewhere. But, much like the Director's race, she couldn't be sure where it was she was getting. And it was in just such a state of mind that she found herself in a huge meeting room. She heard someone scream, "Off with their budget – 10 percent!" At the front of the room was the Chief (that is, the Chief Executive Officer), bright red from screaming. "Off with their budget – 10 percent!" Alice realized she was standing next to three quivering Executives. "What is happening?" she asked.

One Executive turned to her and said, "The Chief has determined how we will succeed next year."

"And how will that be accomplished?" asked Alice.

"Can't you hear him," answered the Executive. And, at that moment, the Chief yelled again, "Off with their budget – 10 percent!" The Executive went on, "He is talking to each of the Executives and letting them know his expectations for next year. Oh dear, I'm sorry. I must leave now. It is my turn." And the Executive headed towards the Chief. "Sir, I am the Executive in charge of Human Resources and if we have to cut the budget again this year we will not be able to provide service to the employees."

"Off with their budget – 10 percent!" the Chief screamed, and his assistant typed a very important looking note in an even more important looking computer. The Executive in charge of Human Resources walked away with his head hanging low.

The next Executive approached the Chief. "Sir, I am the Executive in charge of Building Operations, and I barely have enough money to keep the lights on. If I am forced to cut my budget, the offices will have to be completely dark for two hours every day."

"Off with their budget – 10 percent!" the Chief screamed, followed by additional important typing from the assistant.

"But sir," said the Executive, and everyone in the room stopped breathing. No one had argued with the Chief all day. "My entire department's budget is as much as one small sales promotion from the

Marketing Department. Would it not be possible for me to keep my budget and Marketing to remove that one promotion?"

The Chief grew redder. "I have decreed that every budget must be cut by 10 percent. There are no exceptions. There are no differences. You will cut your budget by 10 percent. Off with their budget – 10 percent!"

Alice turned to the last Executive. "Isn't a leader supposed to have vision?"

He smiled at her kindly. "I remember when I had naïve views of the world; when I was fresh from graduation. Of course he has vision. We are seeing his vision right now. We can succeed if we all just cut our budgets by 10 percent. What more vision do you need?"

Alice could bear to watch no longer. Turning to run from the CEO, she ran straight into a wall. Picking herself up, she realized she was back in the reception lounge. She looked at the lobby. She looked at the receptionist and guard. She looked at the company newsletter. And she never looked back as she left without an interview.

—AUDITORS—
ANONYMOUS

"My name is Bob – and I am an auditor."

"Hi, Bob."

"It's been 47 days since my last audit. It started innocently enough – just a small audit – just a review of petty cash. But, before I knew it, I was out of control. I was verifying cash collections on office football pools. I was ticking and tying reconciliations – even the reconciliations of failing relationships!

The last thing I remember, I had a spreadsheet in each hand, two clients in the room, and 15 computer reports – trying to make all the data match. I woke up two weeks later with a completed audit report in my hands, the taste of ink in my mouth, and a vague recollection of getting people terminated for signing authorizations using initials instead of their full names. ('But I thought your actual name was Bradford T. Wordsworth III!')"

It's Bob's first Auditors Anonymous meeting and, unfortunately, his is a typical story. Sure, he started out doing a few audits just for the fun of it – performing a quick review, asking a few questions. Maybe he prepared a few statements just for kicks, ignoring the next morning's writer's cramp.

But soon it was an obsession – a need for that adrenaline rush of being in control, but not really accountable.

And there are thousands just like Bob: People who thought they were auditing for controls, but finally realized it was the audit that controlled them.

For example, Phyllis started out volunteering at her children's school by helping prepare a budget, then realized she was spending 20 hours a day auditing every expense – and her kids had left for college 10 years ago. And Jeff agreed to look over the meeting minutes for his homeowners association's meetings, and eventually found himself hung in effigy at the local park.

You could be one of the many people who, on the outside, appear to be leading normal lives of quiet acceptance, but on the inside live with the lust to question every detail of every transaction. It could be time to start asking yourself, "Am I an auditor?"

The people around you can provide hints that there is a problem you don't recognize even while they are providing excuses for your behavior. Your friends may say things like, "Oh, we always do a few audits, for old times' sake." Your neighbors may say, "I've seen him do a few audits, but we all have our vices."

And your co-workers might add, "Sure, he does an audit now and then, but it's part of his job. Hey, everyone has to do an audit to get ahead. Anyone who doesn't do one isn't considered part of the gang." These friends may only be facilitators, helping you rationalize the problem you can't quite see.

There are no easy answers. You may be the last one to realize you're an auditor. But take the following test; it may help you decide.

- Do you ever wake up in the morning and feel you can't get up without performing an audit?

- Have you ever decided to stop doing audits for a week or two, but found yourself desk-deep in workpapers after only a couple of days?

- Do you envy people who can audit without getting into trouble?

- Do you miss Y2K ?

- Has your auditing caused you trouble at home?

- Do you hide audits around the house?

- Do you tell yourself you can stop auditing any time you want, you just don't want to yet?

- Have you missed any holidays or vacations because of auditing?

- Have you ever felt that your life would be better if you did not audit?

- Do you find risk assessments lying around the office, but don't remember completing them?

- Do you wish people would mind their own business when it comes to your audits?

- Do you know the full names of every audit committee member, but struggle to remember your spouse's?

If you answered "yes" to four or more of these questions, you are probably an auditor.

It is nothing to be ashamed of. You probably know other auditors and aren't even aware of it. They have learned to control themselves. You can, too.
If you think you are an auditor, it is in everyone's best interest for you to get help now. Make the right choice, and you can once again become a productive member of society. Otherwise, you may find yourself on a street corner holding a sign that says, "Will audit for food."

A PROPOSAL FOR
THE STANDARDS

The IIA's International Standards for the Professional Practices Framework (Standards) exist as the foundation for what we, as auditors, do. Without this important document, the audit profession could easily fall into chaos. We cannot have enough rules and procedures.

In that regard, I have noticed a lack of procedures and policies regarding the use of tick marks in workpapers in general, and the category of tick mark legends specifically. Accordingly, I would like to submit the following to be included in the updated *Standards*.

TICK MARK LEGEND
Once upon a time there was a tick. This tick was named Al. Al was a happy tick who lived on a ranch. In fact, it was a sheep ranch. I guess you could say that Al lived off the fat of the lamb.

Anyway, this tick named Al liked to visit his friends all over the ranch. Sometimes he'd visit George who lived on the horse. Or he'd visit Louis who lived on the dog. But his favorite friend was Dee. Dee was his girlfriend. She lived on the ranch's cat. Al thought she was the most gorgeous creature on the farm. And he thought she had the cutest tail of any tick he had ever met.

As you may know, every good legend needs some tragedy, and Al's story is no different. You see, one day he was on his way to visit Dee when there was a horrible hailstorm. Braving the turbulent wind and rain, he struggled to where he knew the cat always hid during storms. But when he reached the old porch, he found that it had been destroyed by hail the size of grapefruits, which is always more deadly than grapefruit the size of hail. Digging through the rubble or, more accurately, burrowing through the rubble, Al found the battered body of the ranch cat. His hopes were completely dashed when, climbing aboard the cat, he heard Dee's dying words, "Remember our love."

Al returned to his lamb, crying Dee's name. All his friends tried to console him, but he just brushed them aside. He knew he'd always remember their love, but he wanted the world to remember it also.

A few days later, he learned that auditors from the insurance company were coming to the ranch to review the loss that the company had declared a catastrophe. This "cat" team was required to inspect all cat losses. It seemed to Al that they should be just as concerned about tick losses, and he wanted them to know it.

When the auditors arrived, he crawled to where they were working. While they were distracted, he climbed onto a blank sheet of paper. Working between a pen they had left beside their work and the papers themselves, Al began spelling out his love for Dee. Just as he finished the last period, the auditors returned and closed up their workpapers. Al never had a chance. When the auditors returned to their office, they found the story of Dee and Al – the story of their love, the story of Dee's beauty and cute little tail. And they also found the mark left by Al's body – a punctuation for that love. And that is how auditors found the tick mark, and their love for Dee tails.

LIKE A

Fine Wine

SINCE
1939

14.5%
FINDINGS

Welcome to the latest edition of Audit Tasting Today. For those of you who are new to our little oasis, we have established this hideaway to allow like-minded connoisseurs of well-crafted audit reports to meet and share their love of the finer attributes of writing done well. Today, we sample a selection of reports and review some reader questions and comments from the mailbag.

First, to the reports. I'd like to share some thoughts on three recent offerings – an eclectic selection that includes the sublime and, unfortunately, the sub-par. In sampling these reports I have considered the fundamentals of report tasting: the presentation, the substance, the overall bouquet, and that lingering aftertaste that can ruin even the finest experience. With each report, these attributes collectively tell us whether the offering is a vintage we want to remember or one we will relegate to the "Two-Buck Chuck" file.

The first selection before us is a light report from an upstart audit shop nestled in the hills of Napa Valley. A new vintage, this 2007 report is an excellent starter for any occasion – whether you are just entertaining friends over a patio discussion or planning a long night of report reading. When I first opened the report, I was a bit underwhelmed – it seemed devoid of substance. But the report's subtlety soon overcame my initial fears – a hint of partnership blended with the scent of perseverance. So, what started as an unassuming report eventually took on the robust expressions one generally desires in fine reporting. Clear, cool, and refreshing, my palette leapt to the new and exciting findings within.

Next up is a darker, more full-bodied report. Syracuse is one of the hidden gems of report writing, and this deep, complex vintage from that region does not fail. I was immediately assaulted by the woodiness upon which this report was built, sharply distinguishing it from the electronic variety. I found a well-crafted page-turner that continued to draw me in with its overtones of spice and innovation. Yet underlying these qualities was the continuous theme of victory – of an audit report that knew what it wanted to accomplish and did so with unabashed bravado. This is not a report for the neophyte, nor is it one for the feint of heart. But for the experienced reader – the individual who enjoys a report that comes at you full throttle with a promise to take no prisoners – this will be a taste and a memory that lingers long after the last word is read.

After these two successes, I looked forward to that rare triple crown – three successes in one review. But if the prior reports were 90+ point successes, the third was pointless. It suffered from several issues. In particular, this 2004 vintage had aged far too long. The bright, crisp presentation held promise, but the hint of decay quickly became overwhelming. I continued on and ventured into continued disappointment. The legs were too weak, the body too long, and the nose all out of joint. The report was a mishmash of ideas trying to combine the light humor of honey with the heavy pungency of vinegar. Neither fish nor fowl, neither report nor memo, this document left the reader feeling homegrown writing would serve just as well as this pretentious conglomerate of auditese.

And so, with two successes and one failure under our proverbial belts, on to the mailbag. An e-mail from Auditlover32 asks, "I am a relative neophyte in the world of reports and trying to build a reference library. Can you suggest some must-have books?" Well Auditlover32, there are many audit books out there. Several choice texts top my reading list.

For the history of report writing and tasting, you can't go wrong with *From Green Eyeshades to Consultants: The History of Fine Audit Reports*. This book explains everything you need to know about auditing's history and evolution, as well as how the art of report tasting progressed through these changes. The absolute bible on the fine art of report writing in your own home is *From Meeting to Report: The Complete Guide to Growing Findings and Making Your Own Audit Reports*. For a compendium of audit reports ripe to be tasted, either of two books will do nicely: *The Report Tasting Guide for Everyone* or T*he Oxford Companion to Audit Reports*.

And for pure entertainment – stories of the joys, laughter, and foibles that make up the report-tasting community – one can never go wrong with *Adventures in the Audit Report Cellar*. Finally, if you are a true neophyte and are just trying to sort your Audit Noir from your ZenFinding, go with *The Dummy's Guide to Audit Reports*.

The next question comes from FoodFan. "I still have trouble determining the correct audit report for meetings. Is it wrong to have a bold report with a light stand-up affair? Am I the source of a monumental faux pas by providing a crisp report with a heavy presentation? Help me out on these."

FoodFan, you have perfectly stated the mistakes most people make. Light meetings are best complemented with light reports; heavy meetings are best complemented with darker reports. However, never underestimate the surprise and delight of changing up these rules. Nothing can brighten the pallor of a dead meeting like bringing in a lively report. So the most important rule is to serve the report you like – that way, at least somebody will appreciate it.

And that is all for this installment. Join us next week when we explore a nice selection of newly vinted audit reports that stretch our preconceptions about internal auditing. Here's a hint – think consultant and valued partner. Until then, open up that audit report you've been saving for a special occasion and call over a few friends. Because that's what report tasting is really all about – sharing the good times that are at the core of fine, quality auditing.

You Might Be an
IRRITATING AUDITOR

Even your best friends won't tell you. But there is a chance you suffer from the heartbreak of being an irritating auditor. Below, a list of symptoms.

If you believe value add means four findings gets you a fifth one free...
You might be an irritating auditor.

If you tell people it's okay to share their passwords because you are the auditor, and then write them up for a computer security violation...
You might be an irritating auditor.

If you constantly brag that you passed the CIA on your first try...
You might be an irritating auditor.

If you start every kick-off meeting with "You're here because the audit charter says you have to be"...
You might be an irritating auditor.

If you've ever written up your wife for writing checks, making deposits, and reconciling the bank account...
You might be an irritating auditor.

If you start every interview with "Do you know what you were doing wrong?"...

You might be an irritating auditor.

If your cellphone ringtone is a police siren...

You might be an irritating auditor.

(In fact, you may just be irritating, period.)

If your Twitter handle is @I'mRightandYou'reWrongNannerNanner Nanner...

You might be an irritating auditor.

If you aren't happy unless a meeting ends with somebody crying (even if it is another auditor)...

You might be an irritating auditor.

If you insist that all audit report titles include the words "Ineffective", "Gotcha", or "Ha-Ha-Ha-Ha-Ha-Ha"...

You might be an irritating auditor.

And

If you don't think any of these are funny...

You might be an irritating auditor.

AUDITORS OF THE NIGHT

Most of the good workers of Carpathian Industries had already gone home. The sun had set, and twilight cast a glow across the land. Inside the offices, only the brave and foolhardy continued to work. Overtime was for suckers – and for those who had no fear of the night.

Nestled deep within the fourth floor, Lucy sat listening to her manager, Mr. Helsing. With his thick glasses, everyone called him "the professor" rather than his given name – Van. "I am worried about you my dear. You seem very lethargic of late," the professor said. "Your focus seems to have changed – as if you are still a part of the company, but not a part of the business we conduct." He waited, but she said nothing in reply. "You seem more independent, yet quiet, reserved, objectively reviewing all that goes on around you." He studied her closer. What was that he saw? "What are those marks on your neck?" he asked her sharply.

She reached up and quickly pulled her hair over them. Looking down at her feet she whispered, "They are not an issue, barely worth observing." Her language was strange, as if from a realm that was outside the standard reporting structure.

She seemed to gather strength from the darkness. She looked back up at the professor and stared. He knew she had never learned interview techniques, never been schooled in interrogation, but it was as if some dark skill was coming forward, and she realized the value in allowing the interviewee the chance to talk – learning more by listening.

The professor shifted nervously as the emptiness stretched. He felt compelled to fill the silence. "I am worried about you working so closely with Victor. He claims to be a consultant, but there is something more there – he is trying to do more."

"Whatever do you mean?" Lucy asked innocently.

The professor was unable to determine her level of sincerity. "In those meetings he leads, has he ever talked about … controls?"

She returned his glare coolly. "They are self-assessment meetings. Every good consultant uses such an approach. And there can be no self-assessment without some discussion of controls."

The silence stretched again. The professor was running out of ways to broach the subject. Sometimes the best approach was to face things head on. "But what is he asking? Is he really consulting, or is he…" – the walls of the room seemed to breathe with anticipation – "… auditing?"

There he had finally said it. And the word hung in the room like an open-ended ICQ. He watched Lucy closely. She did not flinch. He had hoped she would be shocked, but she had no reaction. "What do you know of the auditors, my dear?"

"Nothing," she replied meekly. "Just what one hears in the halls – that they lurk in the shadows, trying to draw life from the employees who do the real work of the company."

He shook his head sadly. "There is so much more. I have studied auditors for most of my life – have helped root them out of their cubicles. I know their strengths – and their weaknesses." Lucy watched him mutely, but there was anticipation in her eyes. It was the first sign of interest she had shown in days, but the professor was not sure the interest was healthy. "Does Victor have any mirrors in his office?" She didn't answer, so he went on. "Auditors do not like mirrors. They can reflect nothing back to the company. They are only happy when others are forced to look into themselves.

"Further, they cannot come into your department unless you ask them. They may appear in the guise of a consultant. They will try to tell you they are there to help you. But as soon as they enter your department, they will start documenting everything. They will give you engagement letters and wave audit charters in your face that force you to comply. And they will not leave until they have sucked all the information from you."

Lucy sat in rapt attention. It had been a long day, and the professor was feeling tired. He had spent most of the day talking with Lucy, trying to break through, yet there were still dangers he had to share with her. "There are only two ways to kill an auditor. The first is to bring him or her into the light. Auditors live in the dark – their own reality, their own sense of right and wrong. But their convictions will melt in the light of reason.

"You will find that the second solution is the most effective. Locate their resting place – where they do their unholy work. Then, when the entire department is in the field, sneak in and burn all of their workpapers. Without documentation they are powerless."

"Surely, short of their destruction, aren't there other ways to ward them off?" Lucy asked.

He knew she was testing him. He felt an unhealthy urge to comply. "In an emergency, there is really only one way to drive them away. Your absolute last approach is to show them there is a power greater than their charter.

Hold up four fingers – the sign of the Big Four. Then simply utter one word – 'outsourcing.'" She trembled slightly. "This will remind them that they are not eternal."

He paused for a moment. Deep inside, he knew he should be asking more questions, but he couldn't keep from talking. He told himself it was strictly for Lucy's protection. If she were playing with the dark audit forces, then she would need all the information he had.

"Internal auditors must increase their numbers to spread their unholy gospel of controls. Therefore, they select certain people to bring into the fold. They paint a pretty picture – promises of pass-through programs to management, the ability to work across the company, hints of forbidden knowledge known only to the mysterious audit committee. With each visit, they suck a little more knowledge from the neophyte and slowly implant their own ways. Finally, the convert is no longer able to provide value to the company. That is what scares me about your marks – they smell faintly of paper cuts."

He stopped. He was feeling incredibly weak – like he had answered every question in the world. Lucy was looking out the office door. The professor turned and saw a gaunt man wearing a dark suit and red power tie. "Victor Ladd. What are you doing here?" Victor didn't answer; he just stared at Lucy. "Well, don't just stand there, at least take these papers back to your department."

Victor curled his lip and looked at the stack of papers. "I do not do ... original work." He walked into the office.

"You can't come in here," the professor screamed, "I haven't invited you."

"Ah, but you have invited Lucy. It will be your final mistake. She and I would have been powerless, but you asked her in to gain information. Instead, she drained it from you, and now there is nothing more to learn."

The professor could not rise from his chair. He couldn't raise his hand to phone for help. All any manager has is information, and Lucy had taken his away. Like a recent retiree, he was dead to the company. The last thing he saw was the wraithlike figures of Lucy and V. Ladd floating down the hallway.

Lucy linked arms with Victor as they floated to the stairwell. "You did well," he told her. "You are now an auditor. Join us in the basement where we hold our chapter meetings. You will meet others of your kind. You will eat rubber chicken and listen to guest speakers drone on about subjects no human could understand, and you will never have to smile again. And you will live forever – or until controls become unnecessary because people become too honest."

He paused and thought. "Nah, you'll live forever."

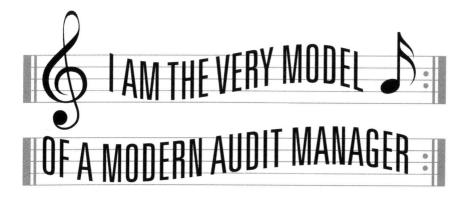

I AM THE VERY MODEL OF A MODERN AUDIT MANAGER

Gilbert and Sullivan scholars worldwide were amazed by a recent discovery in Stanley, North Carolina. An old trunk, found in the attic of apple farmer Frederick Mabelson, revealed a treasure trove of original Gilbert and Sullivan documents including heretofore-unknown operettas, librettos, and notes for future projects.

Mabelson was hard-pressed to explain the discovery. His family has owned the farm since before the Civil War, and the trunk had been in the attic for as long as Mabelson could remember. He told the scholars, "I remember my grandmother tellin' me 'bout some actors stayin' for a night. Course, they left kinda sudden like when the sheriff appeared, so they musta left the trunk behind." Mabelson avows to have no real knowledge of music, other than a few songs that he can play on his "git-fiddle."

Although the discoveries relating to Gilbert and Sullivan's unknown works are fascinating, the items that really have scholars' tongues wagging are the working drafts of some of the pair's more familiar titles. What they reveal is truly astounding.

While it is well-known that Gilbert was an unsuccessful attorney, the manuscripts seem to indicate the much more surprising fact that Sullivan was a frustrated accountant. More specifically, many of the original documents show a great proclivity toward the area of auditing. Original rough sketches of their future masterpieces show this fascination with such working titles as The Mikaudito and ERM Pinafore.

However, the most amazing discovery may be the documents related to The Auditors of Penzance. The notes indicate that, in this first version, the hero was accidentally apprenticed to a group of auditors. Although most of Sullivan's notes are sketchy, one document in particular has shocked experts everywhere – the complete lyric for "The Major General's Song." However, this version is titled, "The Audit Manager's Song." Following is the complete text of the newly found document.

Manager:
I am the very model of a modern audit manager.
I'm known as a professional, a leader, and encourager.
I never come off too obsequious or too monarchical.
But fill employees' needs that Maslow laid out hierarchical.
To threaten or cajole would be to act like a barbarian.
Instead my tactics are Pavlovian and those Skinnerian.
I've mastered motivation, backstop training, and empowerment.
And even think I comprehend the things that Larry Sawyer meant.

All:
And even thinks he comprehends the things that Larry Sawyer meant.
And even thinks he comprehends the things that Larry Sawyer meant.
And even thinks he comprehends the things that Larry Sawyer meant.

Manager:
I've analyzed how best to handle people of Type "Y" and "X."
And have the names of Covey, Peters, and Drucker on Rolodex.
In short, I am professional, a leader, and encourager.
I am the very model of a modern audit manager.

All:
In short, he is professional, a leader, and encourager.
He is the very model of a modern audit manager.

Manager:
I quote the standards, ethics code, and each practice advisory.

I know of charters, quality, and all things supervisory.
I'm very well acquainted with the thoughts on objectivity.
And I maintain my independence through overt passivity.
I speak on risks confronted both inherent and residual.
And proffer that controls should separate each individual.
On governance I understand the various requirements.
And know how best to verify and test control environments.

All:
And know how best to verify and test control environments.
And know how best to verify and test control environments.
And know how best to verify and test control environments.

Manager:
While I review effectiveness and verify efficiencies,
It's more important that I point out each and all deficiencies.
In short I am professional, a leader, and encourager.
I am the very model of a modern audit manager.

All:
In short, he is professional, a leader, and encourager.
He is the very model of a modern audit manager.

Manager:
In fact, when I know what is meant by ERM and self-assess.
When I can meet an auditee and quickly make him acquiesce.
When I can look at documents inside the current workpapers
and understand the steps the fraudsters took in their berserk capers.
When I know more of operations than the chief executive,
And passed each of the CIA parts in sittings consecutive.
In short, I show of all the others I am number one atop.
You'll say a better audit manager has never run a shop.

All:
You'll say a better audit manager has never run a shop.
You'll say a better audit manager has never run a shop.
You'll say a better audit manager has never run a shop.

Manager:

However, I am at my best when everything I delegate.
Because I'm real unclear on how to business this would all relate.
But still I'm a professional, a leader, and encourager.
I am the very model of a modern audit manager.

All:

But still he's a professional, a leader, and encourager.
He is the very model of a modern audit manager.

For the past 50 years, the National Organization of Benevolent Internal Audit Scouts (NOBIAS) has been the preferred choice for every child wanting to learn about internal auditing. In our continuing effort to keep Audit Scouting as exciting and relevant as possible, we are proud to announce the following additions to our merit badge program.

Acronyms – Identify and define at least 100 common acronyms used in the internal audit profession. Rearrange the letters to spell out as much of the International Professional Practices Framework as possible.

Recession – Identify the root causes for the recent recession, describe how this might be prevented in the future, and then provide additional solutions to the federal government because they obviously need all the help they can get.

GRC – Determine what GRC stands for and develop a detailed presentation explaining its importance and relevance to the success of any enterprise. Get at least three laypeople to care.

Online Bank Statements – Review a sufficient number of your parents' online statements to prove significant irregularities. After working with your counselor, develop the documentation required for the filing of a crime report. (The work for this badge can be completed in conjunction with the "Visiting Incarcerated Relatives" badge.)

Social Media – Establish a social media account (Facebook, Twitter, Tumblr, etc.) for the purpose of discussing potential ethical and/or fraudulent activity. Use the information you obtain to identify and turn in at least three perps.

Objective Measures – Define the concepts of utilization, milestones, planned hours, and number of findings. Defend the supposition that "because it can be measured, it must be important" and show how measurable activities, by their sheer measurability, must be more important than aspects such as value add and quality.

NOBIAS is also retiring some of our more antiquated badges including Manual Spreadsheet Footing, Rules for White-Out, From Cops to Meaner Cops, The Myth of the Female CAE, and Bayoneting Wounded.

◢◣ **AUDITOR** 4.0

Welcome to Auditor 4.0 and congratulations on updating your version of the popular Auditor series – one of the most exciting products produced by Compliance and Assurance Execution (CAE) Inc. (Warning: You have purchased the Auditor 4.0 upgrade, not a fully functional Auditor package. Use of this version without an existing Audit program will result in a lack of direction, scope creep, inappropriate testing, and an overall lack of assurance.) As a previous owner of the Auditor series, you know you are working with the finest Auditor technology available. But you also know that auditing is a constantly evolving profession, and we here at CAE Inc. are doing everything possible to make the changes you need to ensure appropriate audit coverage.

Auditor 4.0 offers exciting new innovations while also integrating features from our previous Auditor programs. For example, we continue to support one of our most popular features – the "Independence and Objectivity" application. This application has the unique ability to allow Auditor 4.0 to be deeply integrated within all your computer's operations, yet still analyze these operations as though it were an outside application. How do we do it? Sometimes we're not even sure how a program can be part of a system and yet simultaneously removed from it. Suffice to say that Auditor 4.0 will have exactly the amount of independence and objectivity you desire.

In addition, the "Audit Committee" subroutine is still an integral part of the entire Auditor package. As with past versions of Auditor, this subroutine continually runs in the background providing the ability to override CPU processing that might be detrimental to the success of Auditor 4.0. In the past, some individuals indicated this resulted in processing delays, as the "Audit Committee" program interfered with too many of the CPU's decisions. Therefore, we have set the program to a default run time of quarterly.

One of our least popular features – "Gotcha" – has been removed and replaced with the more user-friendly "We're Here to Help"™ module. The user should be aware that this module contains some minor glitches. In particular, intermittent conflicts may occur between "We're Here to Help" and the "Independence and Objectivity" application. In these situations, Auditor 4.0 reconfigures itself into Executive Manager 3.5 and ignores risks and controls. The quickest solution is to select "Red Book" from the Help menu and run a complete update.

For those individuals who still have an interest in the "Gotcha" program, go to "Tools" and select "In My Day." You will be asked if you wish to run the "They're All Crooks" patch. Select "yes." The system will ask you (more than once) if you are sure. Eventually, when the system is convinced you wish to return to this configuration, the patch will run and "Gotcha" will be effective. Note that we no longer support errors resulting from conflicts between "Gotcha" and the updated "Audit Committee" program.

We continue to adjust settings within the Auditor series program. For example, we have, once again, moved the "Cops to Consultant" ratio closer to a pure Consultant setting. Similarly, with the decreased emphasis on Sarbanes-Oxley, the "Operational vs. Financial" audit settings have been adjusted away from Financial. However, we fully recognize that each of our customers has different needs. Therefore, Auditor 4.0 features the ability to override the default settings and adjust them as you see appropriate. For example, the "Cops to Consultant" ratio can be adjusted by going to "Tools" and selecting "C/C." There are four choices: "They're All Crooks," "What's All This Then?," "Kinder/Gentler," and "Kumbaya." Similar adjustments are available for "Risk vs. Return" and "Ethics vs. Profit."

Particular care should be given in adjusting the "Controls vs. Common Sense" settings. When common sense is completely overridden by controls, your computer system may begin focusing all processing time on working through established controls and ignoring the actual work to be completed. Worst case scenarios have resulted in the entire operation shutting down.

One of our newer innovations is the ability of Auditor 4.0 to explore potential risk and control issues within social networking and social media sites. However, as with many other business programs, situations may occur where these subroutines begin to take over and use up the program's available time. Initially, the user may notice an unusual number of Facebook and Twitter visits. This activity may be followed by a large number of YouTube downloads. When your system begins visiting such sites as auditorvent.com, cybervacations.org, or any sites with references to "hot programs," it is time to abort and reinstall the entire Auditor 4.0 program.

In some instances users have noted that, during the installation process, older versions of our "Audit Supervision/Management" programs may not be completely eliminated. This issue is usually evidenced by "Audit Supervisor/Management" failing to recognize Auditor 4.0 processes such as value add, consulting, or customer relationship development. First try reinstalling Auditor 4.0 to see if the new applications can drive out these old and tired concepts. If not, we suggest you download our copy of Early Retirement 2.0. While this program has a large initial cost, the long-term savings (reduction of conflicts, better functioning audits) are worth the investment.

In very rare instances, users have reported that CPUs may try to override results of programs completed by Auditor 4.0. CPU overrides seem to occur most often when Auditor 4.0 sends a series of inquiries directly to the CPU. If this begins to occur, go to the "Tools" menu and select "Wield Audit Charter." This measure will override any actions by the CPU intended to inhibit the functionality of Auditor 4.0. (Note that Audit Charter is only effective if you have the fully functioning copy of Audit Committee 2.0 or higher. In addition, this program must be completely integrated with the "Oversee CPU" program.)

We hope you are satisfied with your purchase of Auditor 4.0. As you can see, we have taken all steps possible to make this a state-of-the-art audit program. However, Auditor 4.0 is a constantly evolving product – keep running the CPE programs and you should not have any problems. If you have any questions, be sure to contact us at Audit-is-the-answer.com.

CATCH PHRASES
•• for Internal Auditors ••

We can all agree that internal audit's reputation is one that brings to mind such words as staid, conservative, routine, mundane, humdrum, drab... oh, let's just put it out there; the word is "boring". There are many reasons for this reputation, but a major one is in the way we present ourselves.

Think about it. What do most auditors do when they enter a room? Smile, shake hands, introduce themselves, jump right in with an amusing anecdote about the auditor who left a typo in his latest report. These are not the actions of people who want to make a real impression. What we need is a way for people to remember us as energetic, enthusiastic, fun-loving professionals anyone would be honored to know.

The solution is simpler than we may have realized; a set of internal audit catch phrases. Make one of the following the phrase you use to kick off every meeting. Make one your standard exit line. Make one the trademark emblazoned at the bottom of every report. They are fun. They are exciting. And they say, "Wake up, the auditors are here."

By the power of audit committee... I have the power.

Boom goes the test result.

Say "hello" to my little finding.

Boogity, boogity, boogity! Let's go auditing.

Audit 'em Danno.

Let's get ready to hummblllllle.

You wouldn't like me when I have findings.

The power of the audit charter compels you.

Can you smell what the auditor is cooking?

I pity the fraudster.

Hello. My name is Inigo Montoya. You cost the company millions. Prepare to be in my report.

What'chu talkin' 'bout, manager?

To the findings...and beyond!

We're on a mission from the audit committee.

We're from Audit...Internal Audit.

You are the biggest risk. Goodbye.

This audit is going to be legen...wait for it...dary.

And, of course, the most famous auditing catch phrase of all time:

We're from auditing; we're here to help you.

Report to the Audit Committee:
Andersen, Grimm, & Goose Inc.

In the second quarter, the Internal Audit Department completed four and 20 projects relating to the various subsidiaries of Andersen, Grimm, and Goose Inc., including control assessments, consulting projects, investigations, and various other advisory assignments. The following is an overview of the more significant results.

Despite a delay in the audit of Three Bears Homemaking, caused when management was not present for the scheduled introductory meeting, the auditor was able to perform initial functional testing. The overall assessment showed that some controls were too hard, some controls were too soft, and some controls were just right. Management returned as functional testing was being completed. Because she felt the integrity of her work may have been compromised by starting in their absence, the auditor left without completing an exit interview.

An audit of building standards compliance was conducted for Three Pigs Construction. The first house sampled used a new, eco-friendly construction method combining various plant materials. Although auditing applauds Three Pigs Construction for this forward-thinking approach, we found that the integrity of these materials was suspect. During disaster modeling, the building was found to be unsafe, collapsing at very low wind levels. The second structure sampled was built using standard wood

HUMPTY
POULTRY
PRODUCTIONS

construction techniques. It is apparent the underlying foundation and frame were substandard, as wind tests resulted in destruction similar to that identified in the first house. We are pleased to note that the standard brick construction used in the third house sampled stood up to heavy testing and met all basic requirements. Unfortunately, because of an apparent misunderstanding with the clients, our auditor was initially unable to gain access to the building. During this misunderstanding, a mishap occurred. We are happy to report that the auditor is recovering nicely in the burn unit.

We have the unfortunate duty to report a significant governance issue related to Emperor Industries. During our site visit we noted that all employees were discussing the new corporate-branded clothing being shown by executives. The auditors were unable to locate this clothing. When questioned, employees continued to point to the executives, indicating that they were wearing these garments. During an all-hands facilitation meeting, the auditors revealed that the executives were not wearing the clothing. At this point, the executives recognized the clothing did not exist, and all employees readily admitted they had never really seen the clothes.

Controls are now effective at the Seven Dwarves Mining Cooperative. Management had identified a minor breakdown in controls over cafeteria supplies – particularly the acceptance of fruit orders from questionable sources. This issue resulted in the employee who accepted the questionable fruit succumbing to a rare sleep disorder. She has fully recovered and has been transferred to a new position with Charming Cosmetics.

The audit committee previously requested that auditors provide an analysis of a potential security breach at the Grand House Nursing Home. In discussions with management, Auditor Hood noted discrepancies relating to the vice president of Grand House. When questioned, the vice president initially gave satisfactory reasons for these discrepancies – particularly changes that had occurred to provide better service. However, continued questioning caused the individual to admit perpetrating identity theft. Security providers Huntsman and Son were called, and justice was swift.

Auditors continue to consult with Humpty Poultry Productions. Per the Audit Committee's request, we were called in to help identify root cause issues related to plummeting results in the first quarter. To date, we continue work on resolving two primary concerns. The first is determining how the business unit was allowed to get in such a precarious state, which led to the department's downfall. The second regards how this fall, no matter how disastrous, could have resulted in such disarray that even the esteemed accounting firm of King, Men, and Horses was unable to put things back together. We seem to have hit the wall regarding the study.

Our first foray into control self-assessment has not been as satisfactory as we had expected. We felt that a small entrepreneurial group such as HeyDid might make a good testing ground. However, we received no support from the team. In fact, their acts of purposeful disruption included playing Celtic music, throwing milk, and the hasty departures of Mr. Dish and Ms. Spoon. The department head, L. Dog, literally laughed us out of the room. We feel that additional training in facilitation may help.

An operational review of Rumples Jewelry Firm shows that on-demand production processes are working as intended and customer requests are filled promptly overnight. Although we noted antiquated production methods – including the use of spinning wheels – the quality and quantity is of the highest caliber. It should be noted that Director R.

S. Skin may be charging inflated prices that could result in reduced sales in the future. One customer was overheard saying, "Next you'll be asking me for my first born."

However, in a related gold production facility, we must state that, subsequent to our advisory engagement, production has been reduced to zero. Golden Goose Enterprises asked for our assistance to determine how production might be increased. We worked with the head of the department to better understand the inner workings of its production mechanisms. Subsequent to the review, production has ceased, and it is believed that this unit will need to close down. All may not be lost as the department head has begun discussions with Touch Industries and it is hoped that the merger, to be named Golden Touch, can begin production activities again.

In conclusion, internal auditing would like to state that all necessary corrective actions are in place throughout the company, and, in our opinion, everyone should live happily ever after.

Afterword
AUDITING HUMOR – THE ICQ

First, I'd like to thank everyone who purchased this book. Second, I'd like to thank everyone who received this book as a gift. Third, I'd like to thank everyone who stole this book. And finally, I'd like to thank everyone who stumbled across this book in a used bookstore and, unable to figure out how to use those credits you got for trading in The Care and Feeding of Internal Auditors, picked this book up as a last resort. Bottom line, I'd like to thank anyone who made it this far.

Now, I know the practice of using Internal Control Questionnaires (ICQs) has become somewhat dated, but I still believe they can be a valuable tool for learning and sharing information. So, as a special present for each of you, I am including this ICQ about the book. Enjoy, and I hope to see you soon.

1.	Internal auditors do, indeed, have a sense of humor.	Yes	No
2.	I am unclear whether this book proves the preceding point.	Yes	No
3.	The world needs more internal audit humor books.	Yes	No
4.	The world needs more internal audit books.	Yes	No

5.	The world needs more books.	Yes	No
6.	I don't know what a "book" is.	Yes	No
7.	I covered up the fact that I was reading this book by keeping it between the pages of the IPPF.	Yes	No
8.	I thought this was almost as funny as the other books Mike has written. (Wait, those weren't supposed to be funny? Never mind.)	Yes	No
9.	My boss gave me this book and I am still trying to figure out why.	Yes	No
10.	My employee gave me this book and I know why, and she should start brushing up her resume.	Yes	No
11.	I never read the Afterword of a book, so I am unable to answer these questions.	Yes	What?
12.	I am unable to identify my favorite part of the book because it was all so good.	Yes	No
13.	I am unable to identify my favorite part of the book because it was all so bad. {Note to editor: Remove as this will be too depressing.}	Yes	No
14.	I know Mike is Chief Creative Pilot for Flying Pig Audit, Consulting, and Training Solutions (FPACTS).	Yes	No
15.	I know I can contact Mike at mjacka@fpacts.com.	Yes	No
16.	I know that, no matter how weird the correspondence, Mike will probably be glad to hear from me.	Yes	No
17.	I know I can see what else is going on with Mike, his cohorts, and various Flying Pig activities by visiting fpacts.com.	Yes	No

18.	I would like to be included in any emails, mailing lists, social media, and various and sundry bizarre, irrelevant, and obtuse communication methods Mike uses to keep people up to date.	Yes	No
19.	I know that, to be included in those communications, I can check the Web page or contact Mike at the email address above.	Yes	No
20.	I know that, if I love this book more than life itself and want multiple copies for friends, family, and soon-to-be enemies, I can contact Mike.	Yes	No
21.	Ultimately, I know that Mike is ecstatic if I even got one good chuckle from this book and he hopes that all auditors continue to look at life sideways, as it is the only way we can hope to begin to understand what the heck is going on.	Yes	No
22.	I know Mike uses the word Mike far too often.	Yes	No

Made in the USA
Columbia, SC
21 February 2018